Getting Serious About *Love*

GETTING SERIOUS ABOUT *Love*

DAVID L. ROPER

RESOURCE □
PUBLICATIONS

2205 S. Benton
Searcy, AR 72143

ISBN 0-045441-11-8

Dedicated to
JO
my friend, lover,
and companion
for over fifty years,
who continues to teach me
day by day about love.

Contents

Acknowledgments

Since this volume developed over several years, it is impossible to acknowledge all who contributed to its pages. Most of my more recent sources, however, are indicated in the many references in the text and footnotes. One name that appears several times is that of Charles Hodge. I have profited from his writings on love, including a series that appeared several years ago in the *Preacher's Periodical* (now *Truth for Today*). My sincere thanks to *all* who have helped my understanding of love to grow over the years.

Special acknowledgment needs to go to Eddie and Susan Cloer and the staff of *Truth for Today*. Eddie, editor of *Truth for Today*, has constantly encouraged me in my writing. Most of the material in this book originally appeared in his publication. Then Susan and the staff developed the material into this volume. My thanks to each for a job well done.

Finally, I would like to thank my youngest daughter, Angela, for her help on this book. Angi, who has a degree in English and writing, proofread the chapters and made many valuable suggestions for improving the contents.

1
Still Number One!

Did you ever get in the middle of a task—taking apart an engine, a major remodeling job, repainting the house—and suddenly realize, "This is much more than I counted on. This job is much bigger than I realized!"? By this time you were too far into it to do anything but go ahead!

That was my predicament when I decided to do an in-depth study of love. I surveyed all the verses in the Bible on love. I checked the word study books. I read all the articles and other writings on the subject that I could find. I started gathering illustrations. And when I was about halfway into it, I realized it was an impossible task . . . it could not be done . . . but by then it was too late. I was committed.

So go with me as we begin our study of this marvelous thing called love.

AN INEXHAUSTIBLE SUBJECT

One of the problems of trying to do the subject justice is the overwhelming amount of material available. Almost four hundred references to love are in the New Testament and hundreds more in the Old Testament. Some great passages are these:

> "This is My commandment, that you love one another, just as I have loved you" (John 15:12).

> God demonstrates His own love toward us, in that while we were yet sinners, Christ died for us (Romans 5:8).

> Who shall separate us from the love of Christ? Shall tribulation, or distress, or persecution, or famine, or nakedness, or peril, or sword? . . . But in all these things we overwhelmingly conquer through Him who loved us (Romans 8:35, 37).

> . . . Knowledge makes arrogant, but love edifies (1 Corinthians 8:1). (NIV: "Knowledge puffs up, but love builds up.")

> Let all that you do be done in love (1 Corinthians 16:14).

> For in Christ Jesus neither circumcision nor uncircumcision means anything, but faith working through love (Galatians 5:6).

> Constantly bearing in mind your work of faith and labor of love. . . . (1 Thessalonians 1:3).

> And let us consider how to stimulate one another to love and good deeds (Hebrews 10:24).

Then there is the scope of the subject. It includes deity and humanity. "God is love" (1 John 4:8, 16). God

2

loves the world (John 3:16). God loves us (Romans 5:8). God loves Jesus (John 17:24). Jesus loves His people, the church (Ephesians 5:23, 25). We are to love God (Matthew 22:37). We should love Jesus (John 14:15).

It includes every relationship. We are to love our brethren in Christ (1 Peter 2:17). We are to love our neighbors (Matthew 22:39). We are to love our enemies (Luke 6:27). We are to love everybody (Romans 13:8).

It includes every sphere of activity. There are things we are to love and things we are to hate. We are not to love pleasure (Proverbs 21:17), riches (Proverbs 21:17; Ecclesiastes 5:10), this present world (2 Timothy 4:10; 1 John 2:15), the praise of men (Matthew 6:5; 23:6; Luke 20:46), the pre-eminence (3 John 9), strife and violence (Proverbs 17:19; Psalms 11:5), words that hurt and deceive and dishonor God (Psalms 52:4; Revelation 22:15; Psalms 109:17), or wickedness of any kind (Psalms 52:3; 119:97).

On the other hand, we *are* to love God's name (Psalms 5:11; Isaiah 56:6), His righteousness (Psalms 11:7; 33:5; 99:4), His habitation (Psalms 26:8), His salvation (Psalms 40:16; 70:4), and His law (Psalms 119:47, 48, 97, 127, 159, 165, 167). And we are to love pureness of heart (Proverbs 22:11), mercy (Micah 6:8), truth (Zechariah 8:19), reproof (Proverbs 15:12), and the second coming of Jesus (2 Timothy 4:8).

The subject includes everybody. It includes all ages. Those who are younger are challenged: "Let no one look down on your youthfulness, but rather in . . . love, . . . show yourself an example of those who believe" (1 Timothy 4:12). Those who are older are to be taught "to be . . . sound . . . in love" (Titus 2:2). It includes both men and women. Men are told: "Love your wives" (Ephesians 5:25). Women are told that they can be saved if they "continue in faith and love and sanctity with self-restraint" (1 Timothy 2:15). In fact, if you are alive and breathing and capable of understanding, it includes you. All of us are told: "Pursue love" (1 Corinthians 14:1); "Walk in love, just as Christ also loved you" (Ephesians 5:2); "Fervently love one another from the heart" (1 Peter 1:22).

See what I mean about how inexhaustible is the subject?! But we can still learn. Most of us will never be able to chart the depth of the ocean, but that does not keep us from enjoying playing along the shore.

AN INCOMPARABLE THEME

In this introductory chapter, the main thing I want to emphasize is that love is still "number one."

In the New Testament, love was always presented as the greatest of all qualities. Paul put it first in his list of Christian virtues: "But the fruit of the Spirit is *love*, joy, peace, patience, kindness, goodness, faithfulness, gentleness, self-control; . . ." (Galatians 5:22, 23; emphasis mine). In Colossians 3:12, Paul began to tell his readers the way they should develop: "And so, as those who have been chosen of God, holy and beloved, put on a heart of compassion, kindness, . . ." Then the list closes out: ". . . and *beyond all these things* put on *love*, which is the perfect bond of unity" (Colossians 3:14; emphasis mine).

Peter made the same point several times. In 1 Peter 4, he gave a number of instructions and then said, "*Above all*, keep fervent in your love for one another,

4

because love covers a multitude of sins" (v. 8; emphasis mine). In his second letter, Peter challenges all Christians with the following words:

> Now for this very reason also, applying all diligence, in your faith supply moral excellence, and in your moral excellence, knowledge; and in your knowledge, self-control, and in your self-control, perseverance, and in your perseverance, godliness; and in your godliness, brotherly kindness, and in your brotherly kindness, love (2 Peter 1:5-7; emphasis mine).

These are sometimes called the steps to spirituality. If so, love is the last step. Sometimes they are called the steps to maturity. If so, love is when we are fully grown. You can also think of this development process as the building of a pyramid with faith as the base. In that illustration, love would be the apex. Or you may prefer the illustration of a musical scale. The Greek word translated "supply" was used in musical notations in those days; it meant to supply that which was needed to complete the harmony. Using this illustration, if you make faith the first "note," you will find there are eight notes with the highest note being love. Or if you want to look at the passage as telling about Christian growth, it says that our growth will be complete when we learn to love as we should.

John also speaks of the pre-eminence of love. Here are some typical passages:

> We know that we have passed out of death into life, because we love the brethren. He who does not love abides in death (1 John 3:14).

> . . . if we love one another, God abides in us, and His love is perfected in us. . . . And we have come

5

to know and have believed the love which God has for us. God is love, and the one who abides in love abides in God, and God abides in him (1 John 4:12, 16).

These passages by Paul, Peter, and John were written many years ago, but love is *still* number one. When I was a boy, we might have said that love is number one on God's "hit parade." Today the phrase might be, number one on God's "chart." However you say it, the bottom line is that love is still the great need in everyone's life.

This is true for many reasons. Love is still number one because it is still "the great commandment." Near the end of His life, Jesus was asked, "Which is the great commandment in the Law?" (Matthew 22:36), and He replied:

> "You shall love the Lord your God with all your heart, and with all your soul, and with all your mind." This is the great and foremost commandment. The second is like it, "You shall love your neighbor as yourself" (Matthew 22:37-39).

In Mark, Jesus summarized this statement with these words: "There is no other commandment greater than these" (Mark 12:31).

This truth is echoed through the rest of the New Testament. Paul said, "Owe nothing to anyone except to love one another; for he who loves his neighbor has fulfilled the law" (Romans 13:8). Writing to the Galatians, he warned against having ill will toward each other and then challenged them: ". . . but through love serve one another. For the whole Law is fulfilled in one word, in the statement, 'You shall love your neighbor as yourself' " (5:13, 14). James emphasized

6

the same point in his short epistle: "If . . . you are fulfilling the royal law, according to the Scripture, 'You shall love your neighbor as yourself,' you are doing well" (2:8).

Again, love is still number one because it is still the badge of discipleship. In John 13:34, 35, we have this thought-provoking statement by Jesus: "A new commandment I give to you, that you love one another, even as I have loved you, that you also love one another. By this all men will know that you are My disciples, if you have love for one another."

Jesus did not say that men would know we are His disciples if we lived godly lives . . . or if we were sound doctrinally . . . but rather if we loved each other. Do not misunderstand me. Living godly lives is important and so is being sound doctrinally. But when the world looks at us, the first thing it is concerned about is how our religion has affected our heart. I remember one lady asking me about the congregation where I was working at the time. I used that as an opportunity to tell her about our plea to restore the church of the first century. When I finished, she did not exclaim, "That's what I've been looking for!" Instead she said, "I've been looking for a place where I can have friends."

Recently, I read of a young boy who, after being converted, walked all the way across town to a small congregation—passing by many other church buildings on his way. When asked why he went to such an effort when it would have been much more convenient to worship at a congregation closer to his home, he smiled and said, "Them people over there love each other." Love is still the badge of discipleship.

Further, love is still number one because without it, nothing else is of value.

As one thinks of the greatness of love, ultimately he must come to 1 Corinthians 13. We will study this great chapter in detail later. For now I just want to look at a few verses:

> If I speak with the tongues of men and of angels, but do not have love, I have become a noisy gong or a clanging cymbal. And if I have the gift of prophecy, and know all mysteries and all knowledge; and if I have all faith, so as to remove mountains, but do not have love, I am nothing. And if I give all my possessions to feed the poor, and if I deliver my body to be burned, but do not have love, it profits me nothing (vv. 1-3).

Eloquence . . . miraculous abilities . . . flamboyant benevolence . . . martyrdom. Without love, all are nothing! I find that comforting. I may never be a great speaker, but I can learn to love, and that is more important. It is too late for miraculous gifts, but that is okay because love is greater. I may not have much to give to others, but I can give them the most important thing: love. I am not sure I would ever have the nerve to be a martyr. But I can love.

Chapter 13 concludes: "But now abide faith, hope, love, these three; but the greatest of these is love" (v. 13). Faith is so great; without it we cannot please God (Hebrews 11:6; see also John 6:28, 29). Hope is so great; it is the anchor of the soul (Hebrews 6:19). It sustains us. But love is greater. If I said that, perhaps some would want to argue with me. But we cannot argue with God's inspired writer.

The chapter might be summarized with the end of verse 2: "But [if I] do not have love, I am nothing." Without love, I am nothing. If there is no love in my life, it does not make much difference what else I possess or accomplish. But if I can love and know that I am loved, my life is full, and I can survive most anything.

Several years ago I came across an article that illustrates the point. The article began: "A baby does not live by milk alone. No less essential to healthy growth and even to life itself is its mother's love."[1] That statement came from a *Time* magazine. It was a summary of what has become a famous clinical report by Dr. Rene Spitz to a conference of physicians in New York City. Dr. Spitz had conducted extensive clinical research in a foundling home in Latin America. Ninety-one infants were in that home at the time he began his research. Within three months 30 per cent of those niney-one infants had died. The remainder had deteriorated almost to the point of idiocy. He went on in his report to explain:

> It was an old established home, well equipped by all material standards, well run. Its ninety-one infant inmates had plenty of good food, clothing, light, air, and toys. Competent nurses fed and bathed them regularly. But one thing was lacking. The nurses, each with ten infants to care for, were too busy to stop and play with their charges. Each infant had the equivalent of one-tenth of a mother.

"This was not enough," concluded Dr. Spitz. "As a result, love-starved, the infants were crippled in their battle for life."

In another pertinent article entitled "The Awesome

---

[1] The articles from *Time* magazine and the *Reader's Digest* were taken from *Voices of Action* (Austin, Tex.: R. B. Sweet Co., 1968), 142-43.

Power of Human Love," the author, Ashley Montague, wrote:

> We now know . . . that love is an essential part of the nourishment of every baby and that unless he is loved, he will not grow and develop as a healthy organism, psychologically, spiritually, or physically. . . . Scientists are today discovering that to live as if life and love were one is an indispensable condition, because this is the way of life which the innate nature of man demands. The idea is not new. What is new is that contemporary men should be rediscovering by scientific means the ancient truths of the Sermon on the Mount and the golden rule.[2]

It is love that gives meaning to all things.

When one considers that love is always spoken of as the queen of virtues in the New Testament, that it is the badge of discipleship, and that without it nothing else has value, it is obvious that even to begin to appreciate it, we need . . .

AN INTENSIVE APPROACH

In the chapters to come, we will be talking about what the word "love" really means. It is not just sloppy sentimentalism, but rather it is "tough love." We will take a look at the two great commandments and what it means biblically to love ourselves. It is possible that we sometimes hear more psychology than Bible on the subject. Then we want to go into relationships. How do we love others? How can we love our enemies? We

---

[2]Ashley Montague, "The Awesome Power of Human Love," *Reader's Digest*, February 1963.

want to go into the special relationship of the home. How does the subject of love tie in with getting ready for marriage? How can it make the home what God intended it should be? Next we will go to the matter of loving our brethren. Finally we will climax the study by going back to the source of it all: God's love for us and our response to Him.

This study is something I need; maybe it is something you need as well. Here are a few of the values of learning to love as the Bible teaches us to love:

(1) It will keep us from bitterness and disillusionment.

(2) It will develop within us many other qualities we need to have.

(3) It will help us to be loved. It is like standing in a spring shower; it is hard to be in the middle of it without getting wet.

(4) It will help prevent the hardening of the spiritual arteries; it will keep us young. People who love deeply never grow old. They may die physically of old age, but they will still be young in heart and spirit.

(5) It will prepare us for that realm of love, heaven.

Class Discussion and Activity

1. This chapter suggests that love is "number one." How important do *you* think love is?
2. The author gives a list of great passages on love. What are *your* favorite passages on love?
3. Find the section that begins, "It includes every sphere of activity." Take the time to read the passages on things we *are* to love and the things we are *not* to love. As time permits in class,

discuss these.

4. When Paul and Peter give a list of Christian virtues, they invariably put love in a position of prominence. Why do you suppose this is so? What makes love the "queen of virtues"?

5. If it is true that love is "number one" in the list of Christian qualities we should develop, does this mean we can neglect the other virtues?

6. If love is "number one," does this mean that as long as we love, it is not important whether we strive to do exactly what God has commanded?

7. Romans 13:8 is a fascinating passage: *"Owe nothing of anyone* except to love one another." Do you owe anyone anything? (i.e., Do you have a bank loan, a credit card etc.?). What do you suppose Paul meant when he said, "Owe nothing of anyone"?

8. Discuss this statement: "When the world looks at us, the first thing it is concerned about is how our religion has affected our heart." Does this mean that what we believe and teach and how we live are unimportant?

9. Authorities say babies must have love to survive. Why do you suppose this is so? Do we outgrow this need?

10. Near the end of the chapter, it is suggested that love will help us stay young. *How* can love help us stay young?

11. What do *you* hope to get out of this class?

2
The Greeks Have a Word For It

John Allen Chalk tells of a visit to a university campus:

> On a recent visit to Oklahoma State University, a coed asked me to define love. I had just participated in a dorm devotional. After my talk and the question-and-answer period, this young woman inquired privately, "Tell me, just what is love?"
>
> She went on to paint the picture of a serious romance with a fellow student who was now making sexual demands that troubled her. Yet, she thought it might be love after all and if so, what should she say to her insistent boyfriend. The question was an important one to her. It had very real and very immediate implications.
>
> When I turned to a New Testament description of love, this highly intelligent college woman wanted nothing to do with it. She hastily replied, "No, that's not the kind of love I'm talking about. My preacher tried to read the same thing to me. No, you just don't understand."

Finally, I got her quiet long enough to read from the thirteenth chapter of 1 Corinthians. But before I did, I asked her: "Do you really believe this man loves you? Do you think that mature, adult, lasting love prompts his demands of you? Check Paul's description of love and see if you can answer these questions." Then we read, "Love is patient and kind; love is not jealous, or conceited, or proud; love is not ill-mannered, or selfish, or irritable; love does not keep a record of wrongs; love is not happy with evil, but is happy with the truth. Love never gives up: its faith, hope, and patience never fail." My college friend walked away without a word![1]

What is this thing called "love" anyway? We speak of loving cornbread, fried chicken, and Bluebell ice cream ... or country music and Willie Nelson. We say, "I just love that new dress" or "... your new car." We can speak of loving strawberries ... money ... mother ... and Christ ... and go from physical appetite to greed to family affection to devotion to Christ without batting an eye. We use the phrases "falling in love," "being in love," and "making love." Someone has defined "love" as "an itch you can't scratch." What is this thing called love?

A girl comes in from a date. Her eyes are shining. She breathes, "I think I'm in love." Her mother snorts and says, "You're just fifteen years old. You don't even know what love is." Do *we* know what love is?

In English we have only one word for love, which we make do to describe our preferences, our pals, and our passions. But the Greek language, the language in which the New Testament was written, was in many

---

[1]John Allen Chalk, *The Christian Family* (Austin, Tex.: Sweet Publishing Co., 1971), 24.

ways a more exact language than English. English is somewhat like Neopolitan ice cream; we put all the flavors in one box or word. But the Greeks generally had a different word for each flavor or shade of meaning.

The title of this chapter is "The Greeks Have a Word for It." That is not exactly accurate. Actually the Greeks had *four* words for this thing called love. It will be the purpose of this lesson to briefly examine these four words as part of the essential background on understanding what love is. As we do so, we recognize several dangers:

(1) Boring you to tears. Word studies can be pretty dry. But I will try to keep it as interesting as I can.

(2) Oversimplification. Sometimes definitions have been pressed too far and dubious conclusions have been reached. For instance, the idea has been put forth that all these words for love are mutually exclusive— or that three of them are of this world and only one is spiritual. Neither idea is sustained in the New Testament.

Stay with me, and I will try to avoid these dangers.[2]

EROS: PHYSICAL ATTRACTION

The first word is the word *eros*. *Eros* is the noun form. The verb form is *ereo*. *Eros* was used by the

___
[2]In the book, I will often use a Greek word for "love" and then put the word "love" right after it. This is grammatically incorrect because I will generally use the noun form of the Greek word like an adjective. Further it is redundant. *"Agape* love" literally means "love love." Why will I do it? Because I believe it helps the communication process, helps you understand what I mean.

Greeks to signify passion or strong feeling. It might be the passion of ambition or the passion of patriotism. Frequently, however, it was used by them to refer to physical or sexual passion. So we will define the word as *physical attraction*.

Nothing is wrong with *eros* (physical) love in and of itself. Some think that sex is a dirty word, but God made sex, not the devil. God made them "male and female" (Genesis 1:27) and pronounced His creation "very good" (Genesis 1:31). In their original state of innocency, Adam and Eve "were both naked and were not ashamed" (Genesis 2:25). In the New Testament, Paul speaks of sex as one of the blessings within marriage (1 Corinthians 7:3-5). The writer of Hebrews speaks of the marriage bed as "undefiled" (Hebrews 13:4).

The Song of Solomon is filled with rather explicit details of physical love in the context of marriage. Apparently this has embarrassed both Jews and Christians through the years; thus scholars have attempted to make the book an allegory of God's love for His people. But nothing in the book indicates that it is anything other than that which it appears to be: a beautiful story of a man's love for his wife. However, regardless of how one interprets the book, one cannot escape the fact that in it God puts His stamp of approval on the intimate physical relationship between husband and wife.

It is worth noting, however, that the Bible is never crude in discussing sex. Most of the time, biblical writers use the modest word "know."

But although God originated physical attraction and sex, it was not long until the divine ideal was sidetracked. John White has a book entitled *Eros*

16

Defiled, with the subtitle "The Christian and Sexual Sin." The one who corrupted *eros* was Satan; it has ever been his purpose to counterfeit and pervert God's arrangements. God made "male and female"; Satan makes "male and male," "female and female." God put sex in the confines of marriage; Satan says that it makes no difference where, when, or with whom. God made physical attraction as a means to an end; Satan makes it an end within itself. So, as Charles Hodge says, the most private act, the ultimate secret between two people, is dragged through the alley, the gutter, and the barnyard.

By the time the New Testament was written, *eros* had only bad connotations. The Greek god of physical love was named Eros, corresponding to the Roman god Cupid. The worship of this god involved fertility rites and prostitution. This concept of *eros* is reflected today in our word "erotic," which also has only bad connotations.

To the Greeks *eros* was the greatest motivating force and one of life's great goals; it involved the satisfaction of every desire.[3] Some, such as Plato, attempted to elevate *eros* to a higher plane, but it always retained the basic aspect of selfishness: "I want this for *me*. I want you for *me*. And I'm not that concerned about you."

---

[3]"*Eran* [infinitive of *erao*] is passionate love which desires the other for itself. In every age the Greeks sung glowing hymns to sensually joyous and demonic *eros*, the god who is compelled by none but compels all. This god . . . became in philosophy from the time of Plato the epitome of the uttermost fulfillment and elevation of life." (Stauffer, Ethelbert. *"Agapaō, Agapē, Agapētos."* In *Theological Dictionary of the New Testament*, 1:35. Edited by Gerhard Kittel. Translated and edited by Geoffrey W. Bromiley. Grand Rapids, Mich.: Wm. B. Eerdmans Publishing Co., 1964.)

Wendell Broom, Associate Professor at Abilene Christian University, has coined his own phrases for the four kinds of love.[4] He calls *eros* "Strawberry Shortcake Love." "I want the shortcake. I want it badly, and if I get it, I will consume it without a thought for how the shortcake feels." That is exactly how some people treat other people.

Probably because of these bad connotations, the word *eros* is not found in the Greek text of the New Testament. It is, however, found several times in the Septuagint, the Greek translation of the Old Testament that was frequently quoted by Jesus and the apostles. For instance it is found in the Septuagint translation of Proverbs 7:18 where a prostitute makes this appeal: "Come, let us drink our fill of love until morning." The English word "love" is a translation of *eros*.

This is the first word for "love" that we want to note: *eros*, physical attraction, physical love. This is the type of love referred to in the expressions, "Let's make love" or "He's a great lover." It is not a bad word within itself, but if it is isolated from the other types of love, it can be a gross and crude perversion, a mockery of love.

STORGE: FAMILY LOVE

I will mention the second word for love only briefly. It is an important word, but not as important as the others for the purposes of our study. *Storge* is the noun

---

[4]J. D. Thomas, ed., *Spiritual Power* (Abilene, Tex.: Biblical Research Press, 1972), 243-51.

form; *storgeo* is the verb form. This is a love or loyalty based on some close tie. In secular literature, it was used for loyalty to a ruler or a nation or even to a pagan household idol. Since it usually referred to family ties, we will call it *family love.*

Wendell Broom calls this one "Aunt Minnie Love." We love Aunt Minnie and try to help her, not on the basis of her physical attractiveness (*eros*) but because she is our Aunt Minnie. She may become senile, deaf, and half-blind, but she will still be our Aunt Minnie. An excellent biblical example of this kind of loyalty is found in 2 Samuel 21:10, 11 where we find Rizpah standing guard over the corpses of her two sons and other kinsmen, warding off buzzards by day and beasts by night.

The word is found only three times in the Greek New Testament. Twice it is found in the negative (*a* + *storge*) and is translated "unloving" (Romans 1:31; 2 Timothy 3:3). The KJV translates the negative form of the word "without natural affection." In that day, this would have included such things as homosexuality,[5] the exposure of unwanted children, and the drowning of children with defects. Today it would include abortion.

The word is found once in the positive, in a compound word combining the verb form with *philia* (the next word we will study). This combination is translated, "Be devoted": "Be devoted to one another" (Romans 12:10).

---

[5]Some authorities believe that the word either refers solely, or at least primarily, to homosexuality, but probably the word has a wider meaning than that.

PHILIA: FRIENDSHIP LOVE

The third word is *philia*. This is the noun form. The verb form is *phileo*. A great variety of words are based on these two root words.

This was the most common word for "love" used by the Greeks. It approximates the way we usually use the word "love." It has to do with affection and feeling warmly toward someone or something.[6] It was a general word. It could be used of the affection a husband had for his wife or the affection of parents for their children. Or it could be used of the affection one friend had for another. Since this last is a major use of the word in the New Testament, we will designate this as "Friendship Love."

If I like you and you like me, we have *philia* for one another. One of the great Bible examples of this kind of love is the friendship of David and Jonathan in the Old Testament. This word is used in the compound word "philadelphia," which literally means "love of brother" or "brotherly love." It is used in "philanthropy," which means "love of man[kind]" . . . and in "Phillip," which is a shortened form of *philia* + *hippo* ("lover of horses") . . . and in "philosophy," which refers to a "love of wisdom."

Wendell Broom calls this "Bowling Team Love." He

---

[6]William Barclay has this to say concerning *philia* and *phileo*: "They mean to look on someone with affectionate regard. They can be used for the love of friendship and for the love of husband or wife. *Philein* [infinitive of *phileo*] is best translated *to cherish*: it includes physical love, but it includes much else besides. . . . These words have in them all the warmth of real affection and real love" (*More New Testament Words*. New York: Harper & Brothers, 1958, 12).

calls it that because there is a sharing, a mutual exchange. It is generally based on a reciprocal appreciation that can be damaged if one or the other fails to reciprocate. For instance: Let us say that you are a good bowler, I am a good bowler, and we are both nice people. We enjoy being on the same bowling team. But you start drinking and become abusive and throw nothing but gutter balls. The result? You are dropped from the bowling team. As great as *philia* love is with all its warmth and feeling, it has its shortcomings.

While *philia* was the most commonly used word for love in New Testament times, it is not the most commonly used word in the New Testament itself. But it is still a very important word in the Greek New Testament.

Philia itself is used only once in the New Testament, in James 4:4 where it is translated "friendship." But the verb form *phileo* is used twenty-five times, twenty-one of these in the Gospel accounts, mainly in John. Usually it is translated as "love." This is the word used in John 11:3 when it says Jesus loved Lazarus.

Another form of the word is *philos*, which is found twenty-nine times in the text of the New Testament and is invariably translated "friend." John the Baptist was a friend (*philos*) of the Bridegroom (John 3:29). Jesus was the friend (*philos*) of publicans and sinners (Matthew 11:19; Luke 7:34). Jesus spoke of Lazarus as His friend and of His disciples as His friends (John 11:11; Luke 12:4; John 15:14). Christians should be friends: "The friends greet you. Greet the friends by name" (3 John 14).

Another verb form, *philein*, means to cherish and often refers to an expression of affection, such as a kiss.[7]

Probably the most familiar uses of *philia*, however, are when it is combined with other words to form compound words. *Philadelphia* (brother-lover) is used in Hebrews 13:1: "Let love of brethren continue." *Philo-andros* (man- or husband-lover) and *philo-teknos* (child-lover) are found in Titus 2:4: "Encourage the young women to love their husbands, to love their children." Then some forms mean lover of mankind (Titus 3:14), lover of God (2 Timothy 3:14), lover of good [men] and lover of strangers, i.e., hospitable (Titus 1:8).

The importance of *philia* love cannot be over-emphasized. In Genesis 2:18 God stated, "It is not good for the man to be alone; . . ." We need friends. We need people of whom we are fond and who are fond of us. Even Jesus needed His close circle of friends. That is the way God made us.

AGAPE: AN ACT OF THE WILL

We come to the fourth and most important Greek word for "love." Hugo McCord, Bible student and translator, calls this "the greatest word in the human language."[8] It is the word *agape*. *Agape* is the noun form. The verb form is *agapao*.

Unlike *philia*, this word was not used a great deal by

---

[7]The list of the uses of the various forms of the word *philia* could be continued at length. It should be noted that all the forms noted can be used in a bad sense: to love prestige (Matthew 6:5; 23:6), to love a lie (Revelation 22:15), etc. But even in such usages, the word retains the idea of affection and desire.

[8]Hugo McCord, *These Things Speak* (n.p., n.d.), 127.

Greek-speaking people before the New Testament was written. No use at all has been found in the secular writing of that day of the noun form *agape* as a common noun.[9] The verb form *agapao* was used to some extent, but in a rather colorless way. *Agapao* is derived from *agamai*, which means "to admire," and apparently this was the usual meaning of *agapao* among the Greeks.

But when we come to the New Testament, this is *the* word used in the original text for "love." The noun form is found almost 120 times. The verb form is found more than 130 times. This word is used in John 3:16: "For God so loved the world, that He gave His only begotten Son, . . ." It is used in 1 John 4:8, 16: "God is love." This word is used in 1 Corinthians 13, the great love chapter of the Bible. It is used in the passages used to show the supremacy and pre-eminence of love.

Why is *agape* the primary word for love in the New Testament? Someone has suggested that God looked at *eros* and saw that often it had more to do with passion than love. Then He looked at *storge* and saw it too narrow in scope, dealing only with kinship loyalty. Next He looked at *philia* and found even that special word too limited. It was a beautiful word having to do with closeness and affection, but it was mainly for those near and dear. It did not and it could not take in everyone. So God decided to use *agape*, a word without a great deal of character, just waiting to be filled with meaning. He took it and made it the core of Christianity.

---

[9] In my reading, the only reference I could find to the noun form was a goddess named Agape.

We cannot know God's thought processes, but the fact is that inspired New Testament writers and speakers did take an obscure word and infuse it with meaning it never had before.[10] They made it "Christianity's masterword, its inner secret, its outward sign, its unique mark."[11]

What is this love that is so central to Christianity? Though our next chapter, which will be entitled "Tough Love," will center on *agape*, I will say a few words about it.

Agape is not an easy word to define. In an article on "love," the *International Standard Bible Encyclopedia* includes this definitive note: "Love, whether used of God or man, is an earnest and anxious desire for, and an active and beneficent interest in, the well-being of the one loved."[12] Other writers, attempting to define the word, use phrases such as "active good will." Somewhere I picked up this definition that I like: "*Agape* is love for another that is characterized by the desire to *do what is best* for the one loved." For lack of a better one, this will be my working definition through the book.

Agape is not totally different from the other loves we have mentioned. It is not devoid of emotion, affection, and feeling. I make this point because in defining *agape*, it is easy to become clinical and make the word

---

[10]In a special issue of *UpReach* magazine, Harold Hazelip wrote, "Love, as the word is used in the New Testament, was practically unknown in the ancient world. It is not too much to call it a 'new' virtue. Love has been called the 'discovery' of Christianity" (n.d.).

[11]Ibid.

[12]William Evans, "Love," in *International Standard Bible Encyclopedia*, ed. James Orr (Grand Rapids, Mich.: Wm. B. Eerdmans Publishing Co., 1955), 3:1932.

sound cold and austere. Sometimes many of these words are used interchangeably,[13] especially *philia* and *agape* (John 11:3, 5; 13:23; 19:26; 21:20; 20:2). For instance, most would agree that Romans 12:10 has a single thrust, but it uses three of the words we have studied: "Be devoted to one another in brotherly love; give preference to one another in honor." "Be devoted" is translated from a compound word which includes *storge*. The compound Greek word translated "brotherly love" includes the word *philia*. And "give preference to" is a translation of a form of the word *agape*.

The New Testament speakers and writers took the natural affections and feelings of love and elevated them to a higher plane so they can also take in the unlovely and unlovable.

Let me then stress that *agape* is first and foremost *an act of the will*.

The classic *statement* of this is Matthew 5:44-48, where Jesus gives this challenge:

> But I say to you, love your enemies, and pray for those who persecute you in order that you may be sons of your Father who is in heaven; for He causes His sun to rise on the evil and the good, and sends rain on the righteous and the unrighteous. For if you love those who love you, what reward have you? Do not even the tax-gatherers do the same? And if you greet your brothers only, what do you do more than others? Do not even the Gentiles do the same? Therefore you

---

[13]The possible exception to this is *eros* and *agape*. The Septuagint uses the word *agapeo* to describe sexual love (i.e., *eros*), but Thayer, in his lexicon, says that this should not be. Hugo McCord agrees (*These Things Speak*, 129).

are to be perfect, as your heavenly Father is
perfect.

Notice that this passage tells us to *agapao* our enemies. This immediately takes *agape* out of the realm of
the type of warm feelings we might have for a friend.
By definition, an enemy is not a friend. Notice also the
comments about loving those who love us and greet-
ing those who greet us (vv. 46, 47). Is this not a
description of typical *philia* love? The challenge Jesus
gives to us is to rise above that level and to be as God in
the matter of love.

Wendell Broom, therefore, calls *agape* love "Rain-
on-the-Unjust Love." God does not pick out little
areas where good folks are and rain only on those
areas. He lets the rain fall on the rascals too.

The classic *illustration* of this kind of love is found in
the story of the Good Samaritan (Luke 10:29-37),
which is given to illustrate love (*agape*) for a neighbor
(v. 27). When the Samaritan looked at that bruised and
bleeding man, there was no physical attraction (no
eros). The man who had been beaten was not a beloved
kinsman; the Jews and Samaritans hated each other
(no *storge*). The man in the ditch was not a friend; he
had nothing to share; there was no potential for reciprocal action (no *philia*). What was the only possible
motivation for this traveler to help him? He was a
fellow human being, and the Good Samaritan said, in
effect, "Therefore I will help him." That is *agape* love.

CONCLUSION

In conclusion, let me give three quick contrasts

between the four types of love we have studied:
Eros says, "I'm attracted to you." *Storge* says, "I'm kin to you." *Philia* says, "I really like you." *Agape* says, "I love you."

Eros is based on the glands. *Storge* is based on genetic ties. *Philia* is based on emotions. *Agape* is based on a decision, an act of the will.

Eros says, "I love you because I am attracted to you." *Storge* says, "I love you because we are kin to each other." *Philia* says, "I love you because I enjoy being with you." *Agape* says, "I love you," not "I love you *if* . . ." or "I love you *because* . . ." but just "I love you."

Do not misunderstand me. All these words are important. To live life to its fullest, we need a combination of these types of love. But *agape* is the basis of our relationship with God. *Agape* is the basis of a lsting, happy, and God-pleasing marriage, a happy and God-pleasing home. *Agape* is the secret of all lasting human relationships. The challenge of this book will be to learn to love as God wants us to love.

The great example of *agape* love is God Himself. God looked down on the earth. Nothing was attractive about mankind; *eros* would not do. Mankind had denounced its relationship with God; that eliminated *storge*. Neither was *philia* adequate, for men were not friends with God; in actuality, as Paul says, they were God's enemies:

> But God demonstrates His own love toward us, in that while we were yet sinners, Christ died for us. Much more then, having now been justified by His blood, we shall be saved from the wrath of God through Him. For if while we were enemies, we were reconciled to God through the death of His Son, much more, having been reconciled, we

shall be saved by His life (Romans 5:8-10).

God loves us and gave His Son for us while we were His enemies. That is *agape* love!
Don't you love a God like that?

Class Discussion and Activity

1. Look up the word "love" in a dictionary. Share with the class the many shades of meaning of the English word.
2. Since the four Greek words for "love" are so central to our studies, take time to impress them on your mind. Perhaps your teacher can come prepared to class to write the words in Greek letters on the board and to help you learn to pronounce the words.
3. Explain what *eros* love is, and then explain what "Strawberry Shortcake Love" means. Have you ever known anyone who *used* the people he said he loved?
4. Explain what *storge* love is, and explain the phrase "Aunt Minnie Love." Is family love important?
5. Explain what *philia* love is, and explain the phrase "Bowling Team Love." Find the story of David and Jonathan's friendship in the Old Testament, and be prepared to tell the class how that friendship expressed itself.
6. Find the paragraph that begins, "Another form of the word is *philos*, . . ." Read the passages on being a friend. How important is it to have friends?
7. Explain (as best you can) what *agape* love is, and

explain the phrase "Rain-on-the-Unjust Love."

8. To think about (there are no right or wrong answers): Why did Jesus and the apostles make the word *agape* the principal word for love in the New Testament?

9. Underline the definition of *agape* the author will use as his "working definition" throughout the book. Have you heard of other definitions of love you would like to share?

10. The chapter suggests that "to live life to its fullest, we need a combination of these types of love." In class, discuss how each type of love makes a contribution to the quality of our lives.

3
Tough Love

The phrase "Tough Love" will strike some as strange. To them, love is weak, ineffectual, and perhaps even effeminate. But listen to Paul's words:

> That He would grant you, according to the riches of His glory, to be strengthened with power through His Spirit in the inner man; so that Christ may dwell in your hearts through faith; and that you, being rooted and grounded in love, may be able to comprehend with all the saints what is the breadth and length and height and depth, and to know the love of Christ which surpasses knowledge, that you may be filled up to all the fulness of God (Ephesians 3:16-19).

This is a power-packed passage—and much of that power comes from love. Notice especially the phrase, "rooted and grounded in love." Here is a picture of stability, strength, and endurance. There is no weakness in true love.

Several years ago while I was in a bookstore, I got

excited when I saw a book with the title *Tough Love*.[1] Here was a book on *agape* love! Then I saw the subtitle and had a letdown: "How Parents Can Deal With Drug Abuse." I found that it told about the Palmer Drug Abuse Program, which originated in Houston, Texas, and mostly gave case studies. "So it's not on love after all," I thought. But I bought the book anyway. As I read it, I had second thoughts. It did tell about love, tough love.

It starts with the scene of a boy named Ted in jail on a drug charge. His parents bail him out and then berate him. No one is happy. The author says, "If they read this book, it is likely they will not go to the jail at all the next time Ted is arrested."[2] Rather, the writer suggests, their response will be something like this: " 'No, Son. We love you and we want the best for you. These drugs are killing you, so we will not get you out of jail,' they will say and firmly hang up the phone." The author calls this " 'tough love,' a concept that enables the only person who can do something about his drug problem to do it. That person is Ted, the drug abuser himself."[3]

Another book appeared on the market that uses the phrase "tough love," James Dobson's book *Love Must Be Tough*.[4] This volume is mainly on how to handle the problem of extramarital affairs.

The Bible word for this "tough love" is *agape*. In chapter 2, we talked about the four words the Greeks

---

[1]Pauline Neff, *Tough Love* (Nashville, Tenn.: Abingdon Press, 1982).

[2]Ibid., 21, 22.

[3]Ibid.

[4]James Dobson, *Love Must Be Tough* (Waco, Tex.: Word Books, 1983).

had for love: *eros*—physical attraction, *storge*—family love and loyalty, *philia*—friendship love, and *agape*. We noted that, for all practical purposes, *agape* was a new word as used by New Testament speakers and writers. We further noted that the word is hard to define. We used phrases like "an act of the will" and a love that "seeks the best" for the object of that love. Finally, we stressed that *agape* is *the* word for love in the New Testament. Let us fine-tune our understanding of this word *agape* as we emphasize that *agape* love is *tough love*.

AGAPE IS TOUGH LOVE

To appreciate the phrase "tough love," let me break it down into two parts. First, *agape* is "love," real love. If we are not careful, by the time we finish analyzing *agape*, it can sound cold, clinical, and calculating—a computer-type of love.

But *agape* is not like that. In the New Testament it is often used interchangeably with the other words for "love" (e.g., Romans 12:9, 10). John 11 stresses that Jesus loved Lazarus. But verses 3 and 11 use the word *phileo*, while verse 5 uses the word *agapao*. Again, John referred to himself four times as the disciple whom Jesus loved; three of those times he used the word *agapao* (John 13:23; 19:26; 21:20), but once he slips in the word *phileo* (John 20:2). Another illustration is in Hebrews 12:6 as Proverbs 3:12 is quoted. Those whom the Lord loves, He rebukes and chastens. The word is *agapao*. But the same thought is found in Revelation 3:19 where the word is *phileo*.

Agape love is not without emotion, feeling, devotion, cherishing. It is real love.

Second, *agape* is "tough" love. While not devoid of feeling, it is not dependent upon feeling. It is not a slave to glands or emotions. It finds its origin in God—and enables us to rise to a higher level, even enabling us to love our enemies.

We have noted that sometimes the word *agape* is used interchangeably with the other New Testament words for love. We need also to realize, however, that often a contrast is drawn between *agape* and the other words. For instance, John 12:25 says we are not to love life, while 1 Peter 3:10 indicates that we are to love life. There is no contradiction because John 12 uses *phileo*: We should not have an undue desire to perserve life. On the other hand, 1 Peter 3 uses *agapao*, which suggests the ability to really understand what life is all about.

The classic contrast is found in John 21:15-17, in the conversation between Jesus and Peter after Jesus' resurrection. Earlier Peter had bragged of his devotion to Jesus. He had said, "Even though all may fall away because of You, I will never fall away" (Matthew 26:33). But he denied the Lord, and all bragging was gone. When Jesus appeared to the disciples by the lake of Galilee, He asked Peter, "Do you love Me more than these?" (John 21:15). The word Jesus used is *agapao*. Apparently Peter, crushed in spirit, was not willing to use as strong a word as *agapao*. He replied, "Yes, Lord; You know that I love [*phileo*] You." Jesus asked again, "Do you love [*agapao*] Me?" and again Peter replied, "You know that I love [*phileo*] You" (John 21:16). Jesus asked the question a third time, but this time He used Peter's choice of words as He asked, "Do you love [*phileo*] Me?" And the record says Peter was grieved as he answered, "Lord, You know all things; You know that I love [*phileo*] You" (John 21:17). Apparently Peter, having once fallen, was not willing to attribute to himself the high degree of commitment that the word *agape* suggests.

Hugo McCord, who taught Bible for many years at Oklahoma Christian College, suggests several contrasts between *agape* and *philia*.[5]

Agape	Philia
Learned	Natural
Unconditional	Conditional
Non-discriminating	Discriminating
Based on the will	Based on emotions
Esteems and prizes	Likes and delights in
In spite of	Because of
Cannot fail	Can fail

Agape love is the heart of Christianity. It will be the aim of our studies to help each of us come closer to achieving the ideal of *agape* love in our lives, in the church, in our homes, in all our relationships.

THE CHARACTERISTICS OF TOUGH LOVE

Are you still struggling with the concept of *agape* love? Maybe it would help to talk about some of the characteristics of this "tough love."

Unconditional
Tough love is not, "I will love you *if* . . ." or "I love you *because* . . ." but rather, "I love you, *period*." Or sometimes, as McCord put it, "I love you *in spite of* . . ." That is the way God loves us. God loved us even when

---

[5]Compiled from several lists by Hugo McCord.

we were His enemies (Romans 5:8-10). John 3:16 says, "For God so loved the world, . . ." even though that world has so often been unworthy of love. Jesus illustrated *agape* love in Luke 15 as He pictured the heartbroken father looking for his boy—and receiving him back so lovingly. The antithesis of *agape* love was depicted in the elder brother, who said, in effect, "If my brother were pure, if he were perfect, then would I love him."

As I was preparing this chapter, I read an outline I had prepared on the subject in March 1985. In it I found this note: "My first grandchild is due in August or September. I don't know if the baby will be a boy or a girl . . . pretty or ugly . . . perfect or defective . . . but I love that baby. Not if . . . or because . . . I just love that baby, period!" As it turns out, little Seth Honaker was the most beautiful little boy that God ever created. If you do not believe me, just ask my wife. But the point is my love for him was not (and is not) a conditional love.

When I say that *agape* love, tough love, is not conditional, I mean that it is not conditional on what people do. It has been well said that people need love the most when they do not deserve it. Joe Barnett, who directs *Pathway Evangelism*, emphasized this point in an article titled "Hungry for Love":

> No one liked her. She was bad news. Never did anything right. A perpetual problem. Even the compassionate director of the orphanage where she lived was at the end of her rope. Convinced that the child should be in a mental institution rather than an orphanage, the director was looking for a solid reason to dismiss her.
>
> One day another resident told the director the

girl had scrawled something on scraps of paper and tied them to the limbs of a tree in the yard. The director pulled one of the notes from the tree and read it.

"Whoever finds this—I love you!" the note read.

The child had a craving for compassion and understanding. A longing for love. She did strange and irritating things to gain attention. . . .

We all need love. Most of us receive an abundance of it from family and friends. We do not know what it is to be without it.

But all around us are people who have never been treated with genuine love and concern. They're slowly starving to death. God wants to dispatch his love to them—through us.[6]

I mean that it is not conditional on whether we are loved in return. Reciprocal love is wonderful, but *agape* love, tough love, does not depend on such. Many become soured on life and disillusioned when the objects of their love and affection do not return their love. But look at Jesus. John 1:11 says that He was rejected by "His own." He was rejected by the city of God, Jerusalem. He was largely rejected by His family. In His time of need, He was rejected by His disciples— as they sold Him, fled from Him, denied Him. But on the cross, we do not find a hardened cynic. Hear the love in the words, "Father, forgive. . . ." That is tough love.

Unselfish

Remember our working definition of love: It "seeks the best for the one loved." Love "does not seek its

---

[6]*Hilltop Reflections* (bulletin of West Freeway church of Christ, Ft. Worth, TX), 7 April 1985.

own" (1 Corinthians 13:5). Someone has said that you are ready to start loving another when the needs of the other person are more important to you than your own needs.

Love will enable you to do things you could never do otherwise, things you could not be paid to do—things like mothers sacrificing for their children, fathers working their fingers to the bone, children caring for their elderly parents.

Yes, tough love will enable you to discipline, rebuke, or whatever is necessary to help those you love come to their senses. That was the point of the story from the book *Tough Love*. Too many parents never let their children suffer the consequences of their actions; they are always padding the corners and smoothing off the rough edges of life. They are then surprised that their children grow up immature and unable to accept responsibility. This is not an easy matter, but tough love will enable you to do what is best for the child.

Sometimes parents say, "I love my child too much to punish him." And church leaders have been known to say, "If we really love people, we can't administer church discipline." But the Lord says, "Those whom I *love*, I reprove and discipline; . . ." (Revelation 3:19; emphasis mine). (See also Hebrews 12:6.)

Love seeks that which is really best for the other person, not what is best for us. If we are not careful, our self-centeredness can be clothed in the guise of unselfishness. C. S. Lewis illustrates this in his story of Mrs. Fidget in his book *The Four Loves*:

> I am thinking of Mrs. Fidget who died a few months ago. . . . Mrs. Fidget very often said that she lived for her family. And it was not untrue.

Everyone in the neighborhood knew it. "She lives for her family," they said; "what a wife and mother!" She did all the washing; true, she did it badly, and they could have afforded to send it out to a laundry, and they frequently begged her not to do it. But she did. There was always a hot lunch for anyone who was at home, and always a hot meal at night (even in midsummer). They implored her not to provide this. They protested almost with tears in their eyes (and with truth) that they liked cold meals. It made no difference. She was living for her family. She always sat up to "welcome" you home if you were out late at night; two or three in the morning it made no odds; you would always find a frail, pale, weary face awaiting you, like a silent accusation. Which meant of course that you couldn't with any decency go out very often. She was always making things too; being in her own estimation (I'm no judge myself) an excellent amateur dressmaker and a great knitter. And of course, unless you were a heartless brute, you had to wear the things. (The Vicar tells me that, since her death, the contributions of that family alone to "sales of work" outweigh those of all the other parishioners put together.) . . . Mrs. Fidget, as one so often said, would "work her fingers to the bone" for her family. They couldn't stop her. Nor could they—being decent people—quite sit still and watch her do it. They had to help. Indeed they were always having to help. That is, they did things for her to help her do things for them which they didn't want done.[7]

Active

Probably the most obvious way that *agape* love

---

[7]C. S. Lewis, *The Four Loves* (New York: Harcourt, Brace & Co., 1960), 75.

expresses itself is in taking care of the needs of the one loved. These needs may be physical. But they may also be emotional, psychological, or spiritual.

By its very nature, *agape* love expresses itself. We cannot imagine John 3:16 reading, "For God so loved the world, that He sat in heaven having warm feelings about mankind." No, God so loved the world that He *gave*. His love expressed itself in action. When we read of Mary Magdalene weeping at the empty tomb, we do not have to ask if she loved Jesus (John 20:11-18). Her love found expression. Even so, our love should express itself: "But whoever has the world's goods, and beholds his brother in need and closes his heart against him, how does the love of God abide in him? Little children, let us not love with word or with tongue, but in deed and truth" (1 John 3:17, 18). John's meaning is, "Let us not love with word [only] or with tongue [only], but in deed and truth." It is wonderful to say, "I love you," but if we do not show that we love, those words are worse than useless.

Not long ago I was in a doctor's office. As is my custom, I was reading whatever was available. I came across an article in a woman's magazine that caught my attention. A poll had asked the female readers to classify their husbands. There were three possible classifications. As best I can remember, they could classify their husbands as "traditional," "modern," or "macho." After they classified their husbands, they were then asked for the characteristics of their husbands, especially what their husbands did in different situations. There were not many surprises here. The "macho" husband was described as "a good old boy" who spent a lot of time with his friends, who did not pay much attention to his wife, who was too macho to help around the house or give his wife compliments or do things with his wife.

Then the article got to the bottom line. The readers being polled were asked, "If you had a son, would you want him to grow up to be like his father?" The majority of those married to "traditional" or "modern" husbands answered "yes"; the majority of those married to "macho" husbands answered "no."

Those husbands classified as "macho" may have loved their wives, but for some reason—maybe the way they were reared or the pressure of their friends—they did not express that love. They were insensitive to the deep emotional needs of their wives. Tough love takes care of all kinds of needs.

One of the greatest needs is the need for forgiveness. Tough love does not just reprove when such is necessary; it is big enough to forgive. Peter said, "Love covers a multitude of sins" (1 Peter 4:8). Loving mates learn to work out problems. Loving parents do not cut themselves off from their children. Loving Christians know the value of an arm around the shoulder.

Loyal

Agape love is dedicated and committed. It is not subject to the whims of feelings that come and go, but remains loyal to the object of its love. This can be negative, as in the case of loyalty to self or pleasure. Or this can be positive, as when we learn to love God and our fellow man (Matthew 22:37-39).

When we have *agape* love for another, we will be loyal to that one. One of the great biblical examples is Jonathan's love for David, a love that went contrary to the evil wishes of his father, Saul. Jonathan, heir to the throne, said in effect to David, "You be first, and

I'll be second."

In marriage, *agape* love is commitment. Many times I have had a marriage partner say to me, "My husband [or wife] wants a divorce, but I don't care. I don't love him [or her] anymore." What this person usually means is, "He [or she] is no longer physically attractive to me [*eros* love], and the emotional fires [*philia* love] have burned low." But if there is *agape* love, he or she will say, "I will fight the divorce. I'll do everything I can to make this marriage work!"

Agape love also involves loyalty to God. Many books on love have good things to say and important things to share, but leave out the one thing that makes real love possible—a right relationship with God. God is the source of *agape* love. John notes that "love is from God; and everyone who loves is born of God and knows God" (1 John 4:7).

When I speak of loyalty to God, I do not refer to a vague sort of devotion. The Bible is quite plain on the subject. If I love God, I will *obey* Him.

Some misunderstand Matthew 22:37, 38, which says that the "law" for today is to love God. They take this Scripture to mean that if you really love God it is unimportant whether you keep His commandments or not, when the point actually is that if you really love God you will keep His commandments.

> And by this we know that we have come to know Him, if we keep His commandments. The one who says, "I have come to know Him," and does not keep His commandments, is a liar, and the truth is not in him; but whoever keeps His word, in him the love of God has truly been perfected .... (1 John 2:3-5).

Whoever believes that Jesus is the Christ is

born of God; and whoever loves the Father loves the child born of Him. By this we know that we love the children of God, when we love God and observe His commandments. For this is the love of God, that we keep His commandments; and His commandments are not burdensome (1 John 5:1-3).

It has become popular in recent years to say that there is "no law but the law of love," and to say that as long as one has the right motivation and does not harm anyone else, one can do most anything. The result of such a philosophy is described in these words from the Old Testament: "Every man did what was right in his own eyes" (Judges 17:6; 21:25). But the Bible does not so teach. Romans 8:2 speaks of the law of the Spirit, and Galatians 6:2 speaks of the law of Christ. God has His commandments, even in the New Testament. Loyalty to God demands that we keep those commandments to the best of our ability. It is an essential part of learning to love.

Undying

Tough love, *agape* love, is *love that does not quit.* It is a rough world out there. Job said it well in the long ago: "Man, who is born of woman, is short-lived and full of turmoil" (Job 14:1). We need a tough love to keep us going! *Agape* love does not quit. Real love, says Paul, "bears all things, believes all things, hopes all things, endures all things. Love never fails" (1 Corinthians 13:7, 8). I like Phillips' translation: "Love knows no limit to its endurance, no end to its trust, no fading of its hope; it can outlast anything. It is, in fact, the one thing that still stands when all else has fallen."

Class Discussion and Activity

1. Discuss the concept of "Tough Love." What do you think of the advice given to the parents of the boy on drugs? Is it true that sometimes as parents we do too good a job of "smoothing off the rough edges of life" for our children? What can be the result if our children do not learn to accept the consequences of their actions?
2. Optional: Some in the class may want to read the books *Tough Love* and *Love Must Be Tough* and report on them to the class.
3. Discuss Jesus' conversation with Peter in John 12:15-17. What other teaching on love does the story contain (you may want to look ahead to chapter 13)?
4. Discuss the contrast between *agape* and *philia* as suggested by Hugo McCord. Examine each phrase. An understanding of these phrases will greatly enhance your understanding of *agape* love.
5. *Agape* love does not say, "I love you because . . ." or "I will love you if . . ." Give some examples of what people say after the words "because" and "if" in these phrases.
6. In the section headed "Unconditional," find and underline the two sentences that contain the phrase "I mean that it is not conditional on. . . ." Be prepared to explain in class what these two sentences mean.
7. Re-read the story of Mrs. Fidget who "sacrificed" herself for her children. Have you ever known anyone like that? In what ways were Mrs. Fidget's sacrifices selfish?

8. In the section headed "Active," look again at the reference to the article on the three kinds of husbands. Why do some husbands find it hard to express love to their wives? How does this affect a marriage? Can a husband *learn* to express his love?

9. Discuss how obedience to God expresses loyalty to God.

10. In class read 1 Corinthians 13:7, 8a in several translations. How does this passage emphasize that love is "undying"?

4
The "More Excellent Way"

In our study of love, we have been focusing on the word *agape*. The definitive chapter on *agape* love is 1 Corinthians 13, one of the most challenging chapters in the Bible. Concerning this passage, biblical scholar J. W. McGarvey said, "This scripture has been admired by all ages, but unfortunately has been kept by none." Well-known commentator William Barclay notes, "This chapter more severely tests the good man than perhaps any chapter in the New Testament." The reason is that this chapter goes behind what we do; it goes to our *motives*.

I approach this section of the book and the next with some apprehension. Certain biblical statements, verses, and chapters defy embellishment; to add is but to detract. Like the greatest mountain peaks, they are virtually unclimbable.[1] First Corinthians 13 is such a chapter. But since it is basic to our study, we will do the best we can.

---

[1] The last two sentences are adapted from Charles Hodge.

We should begin with some background to the chapter. The Corinthian church was beset with problems. Many of their problems were related to miraculous gifts. Such gifts were given by the laying on of the apostles' hands (Acts 8:14-18; see also Romans 1:11; 2 Timothy 1:6). Paul, who was an apostle, had spent considerable time at Corinth, so the Corinthians were "not lacking in any gift" (1 Corinthians 1:7). But they were misusing their gifts, which prompted the writing of a special section of 1 Corinthians to deal with the problem. This section consists of three chapters: 12, 13, and 14. In chapter 12, Paul listed nine or so of the miraculous gifts (note vv. 8-10) and taught the need to be unified. In chapter 13, Paul stressed that they should not overemphasize miraculous gifts because they were not that important and were only temporary. Finally, in chapter 14, he told them how to use the gifts as long as they had them. Our concern will be with chapter 13.

Let us now go to the last verse of chapter 12. After discussing miraculous gifts, Paul said, "And I show you a still more excellent way" (1 Corinthians 12:31). The phrase translated "a still more excellent way" literally means "a road (or way) according to a throwing beyond, i.e., that which is better." Hugo McCord says this could be translated "a way of excellency" or "a road of superiority." The NIV translates the phrase, "the most excellent way." In context, Paul is contrasting this "way" with miraculous gifts; he will show a way that is *better* than these gifts.

I am sure that all rational individuals want what is "more excellent." We do not prefer the inferior; we would like to have the best. But what is this "more excellent way"? There were no chapter divisions in the original text. So as soon as Paul said, "And I show you a still more excellent way," he begins to tell them about *love* in chapter 13:

> If I speak with the tongues of men and of angels, but do not have love, I have become a noisy gong or a clanging cymbal. And if I have the gift of prophecy, and know all mysteries and all knowledge; and if I have all faith, so as to remove mountains, but do not have love, I am nothing. And if I give all my possessions to feed the poor, and if I deliver my body to be burned, but do not have love, it profits me nothing. Love is patient, love is kind, and is not jealous; love does not brag and is not arrogant, does not behave unbecomingly; it does not seek its own, is not provoked, does not take into account a wrong suffered, does not rejoice in unrighteousness, but rejoices with the truth; bears all things, believes all things, hopes all things, endures all things. Love never fails; but if there are gifts of prophecy, they will be done away with; if there are tongues, they will cease; if there is knowledge, it will be done away. For we know in part, and we prophesy in part; but when the perfect comes, the partial will be done away. When I was a child, I used to speak as a child, think as a child, reason as a child; when I became a man, I did away with childish things. For now we see in a mirror dimly, but then face to face; now I know in part, but then I shall know fully just as I also have been fully known. But now abide faith, hope, love, these three; but the greatest of these is love.[2]

---

[2]If you have the KJV, you have the word "charity" in this passage instead of the word "love." But the word in the original is the Greek word *agape*. Usually the KJV uses the word "love" to translate *agape*, but in thirteen instances, half of them in 1 Corinthians 13, it uses the word "charity." The English word "charity" comes from a Latin word for "dear."

But *why* is love the "more excellent way"? Paul gives three reasons:[3]

LOVE'S SUPERIORITY

Paul begins by noting that love is superior to miraculous gifts because, without the motivation of love, such gifts were empty and meaningless.

It was a common belief that miraculous gifts were a sign of special favor from God. When seventy men who had been sent by Jesus on a preaching tour returned, they were rejoicing because they could cast out demons. But Jesus said to them, "Do not rejoice in this, that the spirits are subject to you, but rejoice that your names are recorded in heaven" (Luke 10:20). In other words, some things were more important than the ability to do miracles.

Apparently the Corinthians believed that certain gifts gave them spiritual status. Some still believe that way today. One noted leader and teacher of today proclaims that miraculous gifts could solve most, if not all, of the problems in the church, that miraculous gifts bring warmth, vitality, and spirituality to the church—and put an end to apathy, lethargy, and ritualism.

But Paul says something is vastly superior to miraculous gifts—and that is love.

Before noting Paul's reasoning in the first three verses, however, I should mention that Paul does not limit his argument to *miraculous* gifts. He wants Christians to know that love is superior to *all* gifts. After

---

[3]The three "S's" are borrowed from Avon Malone.

mentioning three or four miraculous gifts, he then goes to the non-miraculous—the ability to give and sacrifice—and makes the same point. Paul wants us to know today that love must permeate *all* we do!

Paul begins: "If I speak with the tongues of men and of angels, but do not have love, I have become a noisy gong or a clanging cymbal" (v. 1). He begins with the gift most prized by the Corinthians: speaking in tongues, the miraculous ability to speak in a language that one had not studied. This was an impressive gift and was highly sought. But in chapter 14, Paul pointed out that this was limited and inferior to practical gifts such as prophecy (note vv. 18, 19, etc.).

There is considerable speculation as what "the tongues . . . of angels" might mean. Some use this today to justify what *they* call "tongue speaking," which is little more than a sequence of nonsensical sounds. When it is pointed out that their speech is not any known language (as the "tongues" of Acts 2 were—cf. Acts 2:4, 6, 8), they reply, "Oh, we are speaking with the tongues of angels." But every time we read about angels speaking in the Bible, the sounds are intelligible. When they spoke, people understood what they were saying. So-called "heavenly speech" produced today is the result of someone's overactive imagination and highly active vocal cords.

When Paul refers to "the tongues . . . of angels," what we probably have is a rhetorical exaggeration: the ability to speak in tongues (languages) to a superlative degree. Even if one could speak in *every* language, whether in earth or heaven, and has no love, the result would just be so much noise. In those days heathen worship often featured the clashing of cymbals and the "braying" of trumpets. Maybe this was in

Paul's mind. At any rate, a discordant noise is the image he uses—like that of an orchestra tuning up.

Although we do not today live in the age of miracles, we can still make application. Few gifts are more highly prized in U.S. society today than the ability to speak well. Former President Reagan was known as "The Great Communicator." We admire the man who can hold us spellbound with his speech. If one will learn to speak well, it will help him whatever his line of work. *But* . . . Paul says that without love, the finest speech is just so much wind.

This thought is sobering to me personally as a preacher and teacher. Even if I can captivate an audience and even if I can persuade hundreds to respond to Christ, if there is no *love* in my heart, I stand indicted before God, who is love.

Next Paul says, "And if I have the gift of prophecy, and know all mysteries and all knowledge; and if I have all faith, so as to remove mountains, but do not have love, I am nothing" (v. 2).

In this verse Paul refers to several miraculous gifts. Such gifts were essential in those days before the perfect (completed) law came. First Corinthians was written about A.D. 57. At that time about three or four of the New Testament books had been written, but probably the Christians at Corinth had seen none of them. In the absence of the apostle, they had to have the kind of gifts Paul speaks of to know the will of God.

The first gift mentioned in verse 2 is the gift of prophecy, an important gift. All Jews wished that their boys could be prophets. The word "prophet" referred to a spokesman for God, His "mouthpiece"— one who spoke on behalf of God by inspiration. First

Corinthians 14 makes it clear that this was one of the more valuable gifts (note v. 3, etc.). But Paul says that without love, such a gift is meaningless. Balaam spoke words of prophecy, but lacked love for God (Numbers 24:1ff.; 31:8). Caiaphas also spoke words of prophecy, but not to his credit (John 11:51).

Paul also refers to knowing all mysteries. Perhaps this refers to the gift of wisdom (1 Corinthians 12:8), but more likely this is merely part of the gift of knowledge mentioned next in the verse. It would refer to having a great depth of insight into things spiritual. Then Paul speaks of having all knowledge. In this context, this would be supernatural knowledge—to know God's will, without study, by inspiration.

Next Paul refers to having all faith so that one could remove mountains. Again, in this context, supernatural faith is being considered (1 Corinthians 12:9)—not the kind that comes from a study of God's Word (Romans 10:17), nor the kind without which we cannot please God (Hebrews 11:6). This is a special kind of faith that came directly from God and enabled one to do marvelous things. The specific marvelous thing in this verse is the removal of mountains. The "mountains" here could be literal; if moving a mountain was what God wanted, no doubt a God-empowered man could have done it (note Matthew 17:20). But probably we have another hyperbole to get across the point. "Moving mountains" was a colloquialism in those days, an idiomatic expression used by the Jews for the solving of problems. Paul is apparently speaking of the ability to perform miracles of a kind that would build up and strengthen.

Paul lists the miraculous gifts that would have been of the greatest value in the early church, no doubt intending that these should simply be representative of all the gifts. He then said, in effect, "But even if I have such gifts, if I do not have love, I am nothing!"

Again, does not this speak to us today? We may wish that we could foretell the future. But even if we *could*, without love, we would be nothing. We might wish that we could understand all mysteries. There are so many mysteries that fascinate us: there is endless speculation about things such as UFO's, dinosaurs, the Bermuda triangle. Then there are the mysteries that touch every life: death, suffering, wars, trials and tribulations. But even if we had the capacity to understand all that and more, if we had no love, we would be nothing.

I must admit that I wish I had all knowledge. If I had all scientific knowledge, I could improve the quality of life. If I had all medical knowledge, I could cure every ill. If I had all financial knowledge, I could amass a fortune. If I had all political knowledge, I could advise the President. If I had all grammatical knowledge, I could preach and write better. But even if I had such knowledge, without love, I would be nothing. Paul put knowledge in perspective in 1 Corinthians 8:1, when he said, "Knowledge puffs up, but love builds up" (NIV).

I could wish I had all faith, so that nothing would be impossible. But without love, I would have power without restraint. Judas had the power to do miracles (Matthew 10:1), but his heart was not right.

Then Paul says, "And if I give all my possessions to feed the poor, and if I deliver my body to be burned, but do not have love, it profits me nothing" (v. 3).

I might sell my car, sell my house and its furnishings, sell my library and teaching aids, empty my bank account, sell my IRA's, and give it all to a children's home or to the homeless on the street or to the bums on skid row, but if I do it from grim sense of duty and not from love, it profits me nothing.

Or I might make the supreme sacrifice and give my body to be burned.[4] The three Hebrew children knew they were committing their bodies to the flames when they refused to bow before the pagan image (Daniel 3:23). In the first centuries of Christianity, Christians knew they would be burned alive when they refused to deny the faith. Nero forced Christians into rough garments stiff with wax, tied them to stakes, and then lit them like great candles and torches. I have stood in Nero's garden where the cries of burning Christians echoed in days past. But even if I made such a sacrifice, without love, my act would have no value.

How these first three verses of 1 Corinthians 13 speak to us today! Today Paul might speak to those who are religious: Even if we know and teach truth, even if we read our Bibles and pray and attend faithfully, even if we abstain from everything that is wrong . . . and have not love, it is all hypocrisy. Or he might speak to each one of us in our day-to-day lives: Even if we put on a show of being a great parent, an honest and diligent employee, a helpful neighbor and friend . . . but have not love, that is all it is: a show.

As one who works daily in a congregational setting, I must make special application to churches. On what basis do we hire our preachers today? Great speakers?

---

[4]Some writers think this language is too strong and want to use variant readings (see the footnotes in the NASB and NIV and the text in the RSV, etc.), but such flamboyant language seems very much in keeping with Paul's argument that *nothing* has value without the motivation of love.

Great communicators? Great motivators? Great organizers? Great church builders? Or do we look for a man who loves deeply? And on what basis do we honor our members? He works so hard. . . . She does so much. . . . He is so talented. Or, she knows how to love.

Regardless of where we live or what we do, 1 Corinthians 13:1-3 should make us search our hearts and lives.

LOVE'S SUPERLATIVES

Paul's second argument is that love is "more excellent" than miraculous gifts because love, not miraculous gifts, is the well-spring of all Christian virtues.

It is commonly thought today that the possession of miraculous gifts is directly tied with spiritual growth. But this is not so. The Corinthians did not have to take a back seat to anyone when it came to the possession of miraculous abilities (1 Corinthians 1:7), but they were totally lacking in spiritual maturity. Paul said he still had to talk to them as "babes in Christ" (1 Corinthians 3:1) in spite of the fact that they had been Christians for many years. Their problem was not that they were lacking in miraculous gifts; it was that they were lacking in love.

Paul, therefore, pens this section on the qualities of real love:

> Love is patient, love is kind, and is not jealous; love does not brag and is not arrogant, does not act unbecomingly; it does not seek its own, is not provoked, does not take into account a wrong suffered, does not rejoice in unrighteousness,

but rejoices with the truth; bears all things, believes all things, hopes all things, endures all things (vv. 4-7).

Evangelist George Bailey summarizes these verses this way:

> In a world of misunderstanding, "love is patient." In a world of bitterness, "love is kind." In a world of competition, love "is not jealous." In a world of fame, honor, and praise, "love does not brag." In a world of pride, love "is not arrogant." In a world of discourtesy, love "does not act unbecomingly." In a world of selfishness, love "does not seek its own." In a world of anger, temper, and rage, love "is not provoked." In a world of insincerity, love "does not take into account a wrong suffered." In a world of jealousy, love "does not rejoice in unrighteousness, but rejoices with the truth." In a world of cowardice, love "bears all things." In a world of suspicion, love "believes all things." In a world of pessimism, love "hopes all things." In a world of persecution, love "endures all things."[5]

It is hard for us to express how superlative these qualities of love really are. Since God is love (1 John 4:8, 16), these qualities can be used to show God's nature:

> God is patient, God is kind, and is not jealous; God does not brag and is not arrogant, does not act unbecomingly; God does not seek His own, is not provoked, does not take into account a wrong

---

[5]David Roper, "The Greatest Thing in the World," *The Preacher's Periodical*, August 1982, 23ff. This is one sermon in a mini-series on "Sermons Worth Repeating" and is my version of a sermon on 1 Corinthians 13 delivered by George Bailey at the College church, Abilene, Texas, in the fall of 1954.

suffered, does not rejoice in unrighteousness, but rejoices with the truth; God bears all things, believes all things, hopes all things, endures all things. God never fails.

But Jesus said, "He who has seen Me has seen the Father" (John 14:9), so these words can also be applied to Jesus:

Jesus is patient, Jesus is kind, and is not jealous; Jesus does not brag and is not arrogant, does not act unbecomingly; Jesus does not seek His own, is not provoked, does not take into account a wrong suffered, does not rejoice in unrighteousness, but rejoices with the truth; Jesus bears all things, believes all things, hopes all things, endures all things. Jesus never fails.

But a Christian is challenged to be like God (Matthew 5:48) and to follow Jesus' example (Philippians 2:5). So we should be able to also use the word "Christian" in this text. You may want to try reading it again, using the word "Christian" in place of the word "love."

But I am supposed to be a Christian . . . and you are supposed to be a Christian . . . so we should be able to substitute our own names in the verses. Let us read them again. I will use my name and where I use my name, you say your own to yourself:

David Roper is patient, David Roper is kind, and is not jealous; David Roper does not brag and is not arrogant, does not act unbecomingly; David Roper does not seek his own, is not provoked, does not take into account a wrong suffered, does not rejoice in unrighteousness, but rejoices with the truth; David Roper bears all things, believes all things, hopes all things, endures all things. David Roper never fails.

I don't know how that exercise makes you feel, but I can tell you how it makes David Roper feel: It makes me realize how far I have to go to really become a spiritually mature person, a person who really knows what love is all about!

LOVE'S STABILITY

Paul's final argument is that love is "more excellent" than miraculous gifts because love is permanent in contrast with the temporary nature of those gifts. The ability to perform miracles was obtained in one of two ways in New Testament times: The apostles received that ability through the baptism of the Holy Spirit (Acts 2). All others received that ability by the laying on of the apostles' hands (Acts 8:17ff.). So when the apostles died and all those died on whom they had laid their hands, the ability to perform miracles ceased. But love continued on.

It is tempting to spend much time on discussing the cessation of miraculous gifts, a needed study today, but this is a chapter on love, not on such gifts. If you would like an in-depth study of 1 Corinthians 13 from the standpoint of gifts, I would recommend Gary Workman's book *Has "That Which Is Perfect" Come?*[6]

Let us look briefly at the last six verses in chapter 13 and then we will make application.

Verse 8: "Love never fails; but if there are gifts of prophecy, they will be done away; if there are tongues, they will cease; if there is knowledge, it will be done away." Again Paul is making reference to miraculous

---

[6]Check with your local religious bookstore or order directly from Biblical Bookshelf, P.O. Box 821, Rowlett, TX 75088.

gifts that were listed earlier: The gift of speaking by inspiration, the gift of speaking in languages that one had never studied, and the gift of supernatural knowledge (1 Corinthians 12:8). While love does not fail, these miraculous gifts would cease.

Verse 9: "For we know in part, and we prophesy in part." As long as the New Testament was incomplete and all they knew came through these gifts, they had only partial knowledge, partial teaching.

Verse 10: "But when the perfect comes, the partial will be done away." This is a key verse. What is "the perfect"? Many suggestions have been given: Christ, heaven, love. But there are major problems with each of these. That which best fits the context is the completed canon, the complete Word of God. "When the perfect [complete] *revelation* comes, the partial *revelation* [that which came through miraculous gifts] will be done away." James referred to the Scriptures as "the perfect law, the law of liberty" (James 1:25). Romans 12:2 speaks of the "perfect" will of God. In John 16:13, Jesus said that the apostles would be guided "into all the truth."

In the next two verses, Paul illustrates his point. Verse 11: "When I was a child, I used to speak as a child, think as a child, reason as a child; when I became a man, I did away with childish things." He compares the miraculous gifts to childish things such as dolls and stick horses, suitable for children, but inappropriate for adults. Miraculous gifts were for the infancy of the church. They fulfilled a special purpose at that time, but they are no longer needed for that purpose.[7]

---

[7]The primary purpose of miracles was to confirm the word (Hebrew 2:4ff.; Mark 16:20). Once the word was confirmed, it did not (and does not) need constant reconfirmation.

They were only temporary.

Verse 12: "For now we see in a mirror dimly, but then face to face; now I know in part, but then I shall know fully just as I also have been fully known." In New Testament days, mirrors were made of polished metal, which quickly became tarnished; then one could only see in them "dimly." The language used here is similar to that used concerning the return of Jesus Christ, but Paul has not changed the subject; he is still emphasizing the temporary nature of spiritual gifts. James compares the Word of God to a mirror:

> For if anyone is a hearer of the word and not a doer, he is like a man who looks at his natural face in a mirror; for once he has looked at himself and gone away, he has immediately forgotten what kind of person he was. But one who looks intently at the perfect law, the law of liberty, and abides by it, not having become a forgetful hearer but an effectual doer, this man shall be blessed in what he does (James 1:23-25).

The best that miraculous gifts could do was give partial knowledge, comparable to a steamed-up mirror. After I have taken a hot shower and look in the bathroom mirror, all I can see is a dim image. But the completed New Testament can be compared to a mirror without the fog. As I look into the Word of God, I may not be able to know everything about myself, but if I am honest with myself, I can see myself as God sees me.

We come then to Paul's great summary statement in verse 13: "But now abide faith, hope, love, these three; but the greatest of these is love." Note that Paul says there are *many* abiding qualities in contrast with the temporary gifts. In other words, in Paul's list of important things, miraculous gifts were not second on the list, right after love. Such gifts came far down the list.[8]

In this verse, in contrast with the temporary nature of miraculous gifts, Paul says that faith, hope, and love are all abiding, continuing qualities. But the greatest, he says, is love. Even faith and hope will end someday. When Christ returns, faith will become knowledge. Hope will become reality. But love will continue on throughout eternity. Love is permanent.

That is *stability*; that is something you can count on!

CONCLUSION

Texas preacher Charles Hodge suggests that we can get very hard-nosed about love. In economics we ask three questions: (1) Do I need it? (2) Will it work? (3) How long will it last? We can apply all these questions to love as depicted in 1 Corinthians 13:

Do we need it? Verses 1 through 3 declare that without love, anything we do in life is meaning less.

Will it work? Verses 4 through 7 tell us that love produces all the qualities that have real value.

How long will it last? Verses 8 through 13 announce that love abides, love is permanent.

God, help us to see the importance of developing love, real love, in our hearts and lives!

---

[8]In the lists of Christian virtues (Galatians 5:22, 23; 2 Peter 1:5-7; etc.), miraculous gifts never appear.

Class Discussion and Activity

1. This chapter and the next are on 1 Corinthians 13. Read 1 Corinthians 13 in as many translations as possible. Be prepared to share with the class any interesting insights from the different translations.
2. Discuss the church at Corinth and the problems it had. Did they need to learn how to love? Does the church still have problems today? Would it help if *we* learned how better to love?
3. Do some today believe that the ability to perform miracles (such as "speaking in tongues") is a sign of special favor from God? Do some today believe that the ability to perform miracles is directly tied with spiritual growth? Do 1 Corinthians 12—14 teach this?
4. Optional: Have someone read Gary Workman's book *Has "That Which is Perfect" Come?* and report on it.
5. What talents and abilities do we elevate in society? What talents and abilities do we elevate in the church? But what are these "gifts" worth without love?
6. In class, read verses 4 through 8a out loud together. Then read them again, substituting "God" for "love." Again, substituting "Jesus." Then substitute "Christian." Finally, let the teacher read the passage using his or her name— asking each in the class to substitute his or her name for "love." Let several express how this makes them feel.
7. Discuss how faith will become knowledge when Christ returns, how hope will become reality,

but how love will continue on into eternity.
8. Discuss Charles Hodge's three questions (in the Conclusion), and give examples of how love answers these questions.

5
God's Answer
To Many Problems

Consider my key ring. One key starts my car. That is all it does. One opens the front door of the church building. That is all it will open. But there is also one that will open many doors. It will open my office door, Rocky Moncus' door,[1] the elders' room, and the recording room. I want to talk about a spiritual key like that, one that will unlock many spiritual locks, one that will solve many spiritual problems.

Before I tell you what that key is, let me tell you about the problems I have in mind. Let us go to the book of 1 Corinthians. The church at Corinth was rife with problems: "preacheritis," going to law against a brother, undisciplined immorality, association with idol worship, abuse of the Lord's supper, etc. But behind all these problems were inward attitudes at the source.

For instance, there was the problem of jealousy:

---

[1]Rocky is the youth minister at the Central church of Christ where I preach.

"For since there is jealousy and strife among you, are you not fleshly, and are you not walking like mere men?" (1 Corinthians 3:3). But not only were they jealous, they were also proud: "You have become arrogant, and have not mourned" (1 Corinthians 5:2).

If you would see all these disposition diseases on display in one part of Paul's letter, probably the best place to go is 1 Corinthians 12—14. All three of the attitudes already mentioned are present in these chapters. Those who had (what they considered to be) the lesser miraculous gifts were jealous of those who had "the better." Those who had "the better" were filled with pride. And selfishness abounded as each thought of himself rather than the needs of the body as a whole.

Other wrong attitudes could be listed as well. They were impatient with one another. They were unkind. The attitude expressed in 12:21 shows that they were not mindful of the feelings of others: "I have no need of you." They were rude and discourteous. If one was speaking in the assembly and another wanted to speak, he interrupted. Apparently they did not care if their actions made the church a laughingstock in the community. They were irritable in their associations. They were suspicious of each other. They were unfeeling in their relationships.

Stand back for just a moment and look at this list of attitude problems: impatient, unkind, jealous, proud, rude, selfish, irritable, suspicious, unfeeling. The natural reaction would be: "What a mess. These are folks with Problems, with a capital P. How could one ever solve all these problems and get these Christians back on the right track?!"

Which brings us to the key that unlocks many locks.

Evangelist V. P. Black[2] suggests that in 1 Corinthians 13, Paul is not merely showing that love is superior to miraculous gifts, but that he is also giving them the key to correcting the disposition problems that plagued the church there. This is especially true in verses 4 through 7 as he gives the characteristics of love.

For a few moments, let us look at verses 4 through 7 from that standpoint—always keeping in mind that what we are talking about is *agape* love.

THE PROBLEM OF IMPATIENCE: LOVE IS PATIENT

Verse 4 begins, "Love is patient." The Greek word used here is the word for patience with people. There is another Greek word for stamina, staying power, and endurance—in other words, patience with circumstances. Chrysostom said that the word used here is the word used of the man who is wronged and who has it easily within his power to avenge himself and who yet will not do it.[3] How we need this patience; how we need to be patient with one another. Barclay gives a marvelous illustration of this kind of patience in his notes on this verse:

> . . . no one treated Lincoln with more contempt than did Stanton. He called him "a low cunning

---

[2] V. P. Black, *Back to Basics* (Nashville, Tenn.: Williams Printing, 1979), 205ff.

[3] William Barclay, *The Letters to the Corinthians,* The Daily Study Bible Series, 2d ed. (Philadelphia, Pa.: Westminster Press, 1956), 133.

clown." He nicknamed him "the original gorilla" and said that Du Chaillu was a fool to wander about Africa trying to capture a gorilla when he could have found one so easily at Springfield, Illinois. Lincoln said nothing. He made Stanton his war minister because Stanton was the best man for the job. He treated Stanton with every courtesy.... The night came when the assassin's bullet murdered Lincoln in the theatre. In the little room to which the President's body was taken there stood that same Stanton . . . and, looking down on the silent face of Lincoln . . . Stanton said through his tears, "There lies the greatest ruler of men the world has ever seen." The patience of love had conquered in the end.[4]

In Henry Drummond's classic sermon on love, "The Greatest Thing in the World," he says this is love being passive. The next quality is love being active.

THE PROBLEM OF UNKINDNESS: LOVE IS KIND

Verse 4 continues: "Love is kind." Someone has expressed it this way: "Love is sweet to all." Being kind is a requirement of being a Christian. In Ephesians 4:32, Paul said, "And be kind to one another, . . ." For just a moment, think of the life of Jesus. How much of His life was taken up in helping others, in being kind, in making people happy?

Would it not help so much if we could just learn to be kind to one another? So many hearts have been broken because we have failed to be kind. V. P. Black had a story on this point that touched my heart—and

---

[4]Ibid.

my conscience.[5]

A businessman was on his way to work, and he stopped to get his shoes shined. The little boy who was shining his shoes was not doing the job as fast as the businessman thought he should, so he said, "Can't you go any faster? I'm in a hurry. I have an important appointment!" In a minute he looked down, and there was a tear on his shoe. The little boy was crying. "What's wrong with you," the man asked with no sympathy. "Are you sick? If you're sick, why didn't you stay home? I told you I was in a hurry." The boy looked up and said, "No, mister, I'm not sick. My mother died, and I'm working to get some money to buy some flowers."

The man went to his office. He had many things to do, but he could not get the boy's words out of his mind. In spite of the fact that he had many important appointments, he left his office, walked back several blocks, and gave the boy ten dollars to buy some flowers for his mother's funeral.

Is it not true that often we are unkind because we really do not understand? But love is kind. We may need to pray the little girl's prayer: "Make all the bad people good . . . and all the good people nice."

THE PROBLEM OF JEALOUSY:
LOVE IS NOT JEALOUS

The next quality Paul lists in verse 4 is, Love "is not jealous."

Envy is a terrible sin. It is listed with the most

---

[5]Black, 211-12.

hideous of sins (Galatians 5:19-21). Envy caused Cain to kill his brother, Abel (1 John 3:12). When Joseph's brothers were eaten up with jealousy, they actually sold him to strangers (Acts 7:9). Because of envy, Saul hunted David like one would hunt a wild animal (1 Samuel 18). Pilate noted that it was because of envy that the Jews delivered up Jesus (Matthew 27:18). In the KJV, Solomon called envy a "rottenness of the bones" (Proverbs 14:30). Today he would probably call it the cancer, the malignancy, of the bones. Think of all the heartaches, all the disappointments, all the grief, all the sorrows brought about because of some envious, scheming heart!

Drummond said this is love in competition.

Let me tell you the facts of life. It makes no difference what you do, someone is going to do it better. It makes no difference what you have, someone is going to have more. It makes no difference how great you are, someone is going to be greater. It makes no difference how successful you are, someone is going to be more successful. If not now, eventually. And you must learn how to live with that . . . graciously.

How can I overcome the terrible tendency to jealousy? Paul says the answer is love. All of my girls have very special talents. One talent my youngest has is the ability to sing. At one time I had a fair country baritone, but those days are gone. And even when I was at my best, I could never do the things my Angi can. So when I listen to her perform, I am eaten up with jealousy, right? You know better. There is no envy in this father's heart, just thankfulness for a gift God gave his little girl. Why? Because I love her.

I know a preacher who preaches for small congregations. He has a son who preaches for one of the larger congregations in the brotherhood. But when he talks about his son, there is no jealousy in his voice, only pride. Why? That is his boy. He loves his son. If I am jealous, it is because I do not love enough.

THE PROBLEM OF PRIDE: LOVE IS HUMBLE

Verse 4 concludes: "Love does not brag and is not arrogant." The previous quality of love spoke of those times when others do better than we do. This quality speaks of those times when we do succeed. Even when one does well, love feels no need to brag or exalt self.

Nothing is more unattractive than the individual who apparently feels he must constantly be blowing his own trumpet. It was said of a preacher, "He is the only man I know who can strut sitting down." And this comment was made about an individual: "If you could buy him for what he is worth and sell him for what he thinks he is worth, you would make a fortune." In Matthew 6, Jesus spoke of those who desire the applause of men, and He said, "They have their reward in full" (vv. 2, 5).

In contrast with that spirit, there is a self-effacing quality about love. It is humble. As Paul commanded in Romans 12:3: "... I say to every man among you not to think more highly of himself than he ought to think; ..." If I understand the biblical concept of humility, it is not that one thinks badly of oneself, but rather that one does not think of oneself at all. Love is so concerned about others, so interested in encouraging, exalting, and building up others, that it feels no need for self-exaltation.

71

THE PROBLEM OF RUDENESS:
LOVE IS COURTEOUS

Verse 5 begins: Love "does not act unbecomingly."
The NKJV has, "does not behave rudely." Most mod-
ern recent commentaries have "is not rude."[6] One
adds "is not . . . unmannerly" (Amplified Bible).
Another puts it this way: "Love is not discourteous."
Drummond called this "love in society."

Some may think it strange that this quality is listed
along with "important" things like kindness and
humility. What difference does it make if we have
good manners or not? Whether we are polite, nice,
considerate, inoffensive—or just the opposite?

It makes a great deal of difference, for at the root of
genuine courtesy is a concern for the other person and
his feelings. It makes a *great* deal of difference, for it
has to do with the impressions we leave on people,
whether we are the salt and light of the world to God's
glory (Matthew 5:13-16) or whether we repulse people by our actions.

One year, after the lectureship at one of our Christian colleges, Charles Hodge had a disturbing article in
his bulletin. While at the lectures, he had talked with a
number of waiters and waitresses in eating places
near the campus. They said they dreaded the lectureship because those who came to them were so rude in
the area cafes and restaurants. The saddest thing of
all, however, was that not infrequently some of the
rudest were those who bowed their heads in prayer
before the meal.

Love is thoughtful, considerate, respectful, man-

---

[6]RSV, NIV, NEB, Living Bible, etc.

nerly, tactful, and polite. These are considered by some to be old-fashioned qualities now outdated, but Paul says if you are filled with love, that is how you will act.

THE PROBLEM OF SELFISHNESS: LOVE IS UNSELFISH

The second quality of love listed in verse 5 has been called the best sentence definition of "love": Love "does not seek its own." Other translations read like this: "Does not insist on its own way" (RSV); "Never selfish" (NEB); "Does not insist on its own rights or its own way, for it is not self-seeking" (Amplified Bible). To return to a definition of *agape* love given earlier: "Love seeks the best for the one loved." Love is concerned about the other person, not self.

The prophet said, "Are you seeking great things for yourself? Do not seek them" (Jeremiah 45:5). Paul said:

> . . . with humility of mind let each of you regard one another as more important than himself; do not merely look out for your own personal interests, but also for the interests of others. Have this attitude in yourselves which was also in Christ Jesus (Philippians 2:3-5).

It is hard to be more concerned about others than self. Paul says the secret is to learn to love. Barclay notes that basically the world is divided into two groups: The first group is concerned about rights; the second group is concerned about responsibilities.[7]

---

[7]Adapted from Barclay, 122.

Again, group one is concerned about "what life owes me," while group two is concerned about "what I owe life." The second group has caught a glimpse of *agape* love.

Love is not concerned with self; love is concerned about the other person.

THE PROBLEM OF IRRITABILITY:
LOVE IS GOOD-NATURED

The third characteristic of love in verse 5 is stated in these words: "Is not provoked." The KJV has "is not easily provoked." The NIV has "not quick to take offense," while several translations[8] have "is not touchy."

There is no more destructive element in human nature than that of being quick-tempered. So many terrible things have been said, so many terrible deeds have been done, so many precious relationships have been destroyed because of a quick temper. Some would never think of becoming drunk with alcoholic beverages, but they will become drunk with anger— and do as much damage.

In contrast, love is not quick to take offense; it is not touchy; it does not go around with a chip on its shoulder. Why? Because love does not think about itself; it thinks about the other person. When I get my feelings hurt, when I am touchy and have a foul temper, it is generally because I think someone has done something to *me*. But if "I" am not important, then slights, real or imagined, cannot touch me.

---

[8]Amplified Bible, Living Bible, etc.

But someone objects, "That's hard; that's just the way I am (or, that's just the way my family is). It's just natural for me to fly off the handle." "Just natural"? Does that mean that nothing can be done about it? Let me ask you, was it "natural" to allow oneself to be led to Calvary, to allow nails to be driven through the flesh, to suffer all the pangs of the cross? Keep in mind that at any time Jesus could have called a legion of angels to rescue Him. What enabled Jesus to go through that ordeal? Love.

There is a transforming power in love to overcome the traits of a lifetime.

THE PROBLEM OF BEING SUSPICIOUS: LOVE BELIEVES THE BEST

Verse 5 concludes, "Does not take into account a wrong suffered." The KJV has, "Thinketh no evil."

Is it not true that often we are ready to believe the worst? If someone does something well, "they just did it to show off." If someone compliments us, "they really didn't mean it." But love "thinks no evil"; love believes the best. In a moment we will notice verse 7: "Bears all things, believes all things, hopes all things, endures all things." Many writers feel that the significance of "believes all things" is "puts the best possible construction" on whatever happens.

If I really love someone, I *will* put the best possible construction on what that person does until I am forced to do otherwise. But even then I will "hope all things"; I will maintain the hope that the one I love will change.

But there is still more to be learned concerning this

characteristic. As already noticed, in the translation we are using, the phrasing is, "Does not take into account a wrong suffered." An accountant's term is used in the original text, a word related to the ledger sheet. It refers to writing something down where it will not be forgotten, where it can be taken into account tomorrow, the next day, or ten years from now.

Are we not often like that? If we feel hurt, we write it down in our mental notebook and file it away. We brood over those wrongs until, for all practical purposes, they are impossible to forget. We nurse our wrath to keep it warm.

But love is not self-centered. Love is not concerned about wrongs done to self. So love can even put the best possible construction on what is done to self. And love can forget. Love does not put wrongs on the ledger; love "thinks no evil."

THE PROBLEM OF BEING UNFEELING: LOVE IS CONCERNED

Finally, verse 6 has, "Does not rejoice in unrighteousness, but rejoices with the truth." There is so much packed into those words, but let me summarize them by saying: Love is happy when things are right; love is sad when things are not right. And both "right" and "not right" are determined by the Word of God. John expressed this attitude in his second letter: "I was very glad to find some of your children walking in truth, . . ." (2 John 4).

You might think that would be natural. But it is not. Many people are happy when bad things happen to

76

important people. Certain publications are circulated in the hundreds of thousands because of the perverse tendency to gloat over the problems of the glamorous. There are those who make their living going through the garbage cans of celebrities, trying to find some hint of scandal. And when they find it, the garbage is printed.

Again, many are happy when bad things happen to people they do not like, or if it is shown that there is sin in their lives. But God's Wise Man in the Old Testament said, "Do not rejoice when your enemy falls, and do not let your heart be glad when he stumbles" (Proverbs 24:17). Such attitudes do not reflect love.

Let us pause here to make a point. Some do not understand love. They think that if one really loves, it makes no difference whether truth or error is taught, whether people live right or not. But this verse declares that love is in harmony with truth. Unrighteousness, disobedience, and error break the heart of the one who has learned how to love. Love can never rejoice in nor overlook unrighteousness and disobedience.

Unrighteousness can condemn a person's soul. And love is concerned about that person.

CONCLUSION

This section of chapter 13 closes: "Bears all things, believes all things, hopes all things, endures all things. Love never fails; . . ." (vv. 7, 8).

When I consulted the original Greek, I found it interesting that in each of the phrases in verse 7, "all things" comes first. The Greek language did not have some of our ways to emphasize, such as underlining and exclamation points. But the Greeks had their means of emphasizing, such as repetition. One method of emphasis was to put a word or phrase first in the sentence. I had always read these phrases, "*Bears* all things, *believes* all things, *hopes* all things," and so on. But since "all things" comes first in each phrase in the Greek, the emphasis should be: "Bears *all things*, believes *all things*, hopes *all things*, endures *all things*."

In a sense, all that Paul says here has been said in the verses before, but Paul is now saying that there are no exceptions. Love is love, everywhere in every place, no matter what. The NIV has, "It always protects, always trusts, always hopes, always perseveres."

So 1 Corinthians 13, especially verses 4 through 7, declares that love is God's answer to many problems. If you do not have this passage marked, let me suggest that you do so right now. We will return to it again and again in our studies. When my friend, Joe Schubert, counsels with couples with problems, he has them read 1 Corinthians 13 over and over together. It is good for what ails you.

The more I read these verses, the more I become convinced of three things:

(1) Love is not soft and weak and easy to attain. Love is tough and lasting and hard to attain.

(2) David Roper has a long way to go in becoming a loving person.

(3) I can never even approximate the person I ought to be unless I learn to love as I should, can never please God, can never go to heaven, unless I become more loving. So I pray:

"God, be with me—and be with every person who

reads these words. Help us all to forget self and to think of others. Help us to learn what real love is. Help us to become more like Your Son, Who was able to love all men, even those who crucified Him. You do not have much to work with, Lord, but we believe that through Your power, we can become real Christians, full of love. In the name of Your Son, Amen."

Class Discussion and Activity

1. Do you have any problems with priorities in your life? Discuss how we can work out our priorities.
2. Discuss the concept of *biblical* priorities. Include these questions: Are "lesser" commandments unimportant? Are we qualified to say one commandment is "lesser" if the Bible does not thus designate it?
3. What does it mean to "hate" the members of one's family (Luke 14:26, 27)?
4. Some scribes believed that if they obeyed the "great" commandment, it was relatively unimportant if they obeyed the others. Do some today apparently think if they take care of (what is to them) a few "important" commandments, the rest do not matter?
5. In Matthew 22:37, 38, Jesus quotes from Deuteronomy 6:4-9 and Leviticus 19:18. Read those two Old Testament passages in context, and be prepared to discuss in class what they originally meant to the Jews.
6. Discuss some practical expressions of loving God with all our heart.

7. Discuss some practical expressions of loving God with all our mind.
8. Discuss some practical expressions of loving God with all our strength.
9. Discuss some practical expressions of loving God with all our soul.
10. The author gives several practical illustrations of what it means to love God with all our being and to put Him first in all things. Do you think the author overstates the case? Do you think most of us love God with all our being today? What kind of message do you think we are sending to our young people?

6
Priorities of Love

To this point, in our series on love, we have been trying to define love and trying to discover the nature of the love of which we are speaking. Now we want to turn our attention for several chapters to the *direction* of love: Whom are we to love? And how will love express itself in the many relationships of life?

Our first chapter with this new emphasis will be the "Priorities of Love." Our text will be Matthew 22:34-40. Before we get to that, however, we need to briefly discuss that word "priorities."

Priorities are a major problem with us. Many have a problem deciding between things good and bad. But for some of us the more pressing problem has to do with choosing between the good, better, and best. We find it hard to prioritize our lives.

BIBLICAL PRIORITIES

It will not automatically resolve every problem, but

it may help to learn that the Bible speaks of priorities—even as far as commands are concerned. Think for a moment of the Bible's use of comparative and superlative terms. In Matthew 5:19 Jesus speaks of "the least of these commandments." Matthew 23:23 refers to "the weightier provisions of the law." In Matthew 6:33, we are challenged to "seek first [God's] kingdom and His righteousness." In the discussion of miraculous gifts (1 Corinthians 12—14), Paul compares the gifts and says that some are better/greater than others—but that love is the "more [or most] excellent way."

Let me illustrate the matter of Bible priorities: Our body is the temple of God (1 Corinthians 6:19, 20). We are to care for our bodies; we are not to defile them. We are not to destroy them (1 Corinthians 3:16, 17).[1] Our bodies are tools to be used in the service of God; they are to be presented as living and holy sacrifices to God (Romans 12:1). We need to take care of these precious tools.

But let us consider Christ and the cross. Jesus had a choice as to whether He would be crucified or not. He could have called twelve legions of angels to rescue Him (Matthew 26:53). So we cry out, "Don't go, Jesus! If You go to the cross, Your body will be destroyed—and it is the temple of God!" But what Jesus did on the cross took priority over the laws concerning the body.

We can think of similar situations in our own lives. Think of the mother who stays up all night to care for a very sick child. Such is very hard on her body, but the

---

[1]Some believe that this specific reference is referring to the spiritual body, the church (Ephesians 1:22, 23). But even if it is, the passage still teaches by comparison that we should not destroy the physical body.

laws of love take priority. Or, consider the loving soul-winner who stays up past midnight teaching someone because he has found a soul hungering and thirsting after righteousness. This does not mean that God's instructions about caring for the body can be tossed aside for any reason; we are just saying that under certain circumstances, other things may take priority over those laws.

Here is another illustration: Children are to obey their parents (Ephesians 6:1-3). Wives are to obey their husbands (Ephesians 5:22). We are to obey the laws of the land (Romans 13:1ff.). But what if any of these "authorities" tell us to disobey God? If that should happen, priorities come into play. Peter says, "We must obey God rather than men" (Acts 5:29).

I do not want to be misunderstood. Let me quickly add that I am not saying that it is unimportant to obey what may appear to us to be "lesser" commandments. Passages earlier mentioned settle this matter:

> "Whoever then annuls one of the least of these commandments, and so teaches others, shall be called least in the kingdom of heaven; but whoever keeps and teaches them, he shall be called great in the kingdom of heaven" (Matthew 5:19).

> "Woe to you, scribes and Pharisees, hypocrites! For you tithe mint and dill and cummin, and have neglected the weightier provisions of the law: justice and mercy and faithfulness; but *these are the things you should have done* without neglecting the others" (Matthew 23:23; emphasis mine).

I am also not saying that *we* are qualified to determine that a particular command is "lesser" or "weightier" if the Bible does not thus designate it. To attempt to do so is to take upon ourselves the prerogatives of God. This was a mistake the Jews made when they decided that the time-honored tradition of "corban" was more important than God's law for taking care of one's parents (Matthew 15:3-6). On the other hand, what I *am* saying is that the *Bible* itself gives some priorities.

This is even true in the matter of love.

To illustrate: The Bible stresses that it is very important to love our parents (2 Timothy 3:3 speaks of those who are "unloving" ["without natural affection," KJV]). It is important for husbands to love their wives (Ephesians 5:25, 28, 33). It is important for parents to love their children (Titus 2:4). But listen to Jesus' words in Matthew 10:34-38:

> "Do not think that I came to bring peace on the earth; I did not come to bring peace, but a sword. For I came to set a man against his father, and a daughter against her mother, and a daughter-in-law against her mother-in-law; and a man's enemies will be the members of his household. He who loves father or mother more than Me is not worthy of Me; and he who loves son or daughter more than Me is not worthy of Me. And he who does not take his cross and follow after Me is not worthy of Me."

Jesus is not saying that we should not love those in our families, but if a conflict should arise between what our family wants us to do and what Jesus wants us to do, we are to love Jesus more. Luke's account of the same teaching is even more startling:

> "If anyone comes to Me, and does not hate his own father and mother and wife and children and brothers and sisters, yes, and even his own life,

he cannot be My disciple. Whoever does not carry his own cross and come after Me cannot be My disciple" (Luke 14:26, 27).

Jesus here uses the word "hate" in a comparative sense. We must love Jesus so much that, by comparison, our love for our family is as hate.

We are talking about priorities!

JESUS' PRIORITIES

We are now ready for Matthew 22. It is the Tuesday before Jesus is crucified on Friday. Sometimes this Tuesday is referred to as "the Great Day of Questions." Jesus is in Jerusalem in the temple, and His enemies are doing their best to trap Him in His words. Let us begin with verse 34: "But when the Pharisees heard that He had put the Sadducees to silence, they gathered themselves together." The Greek word translated "put . . . to silence" literally meant "to muzzle," as one might muzzle a savage dog.

The Pharisees must have had mixed emotions. They loved to see their enemies, the Sadducees, put down, but at the same time they wanted to see Jesus defeated. They decide to try one more time. If they can be successful this time, they will have triumphed over both Jesus and the Sadducees. They got their best man, a lawyer, to ask Jesus a question. In those days a lawyer was not a specialist in civil law like today, but rather one skilled in religious law, specifically the law of Moses. In Mark's account, he is called a scribe.

So the Pharisees put forward this expert to stand toe to toe with Jesus. They want to give this their best shot. "And one of them, a lawyer, asked Him a question, testing Him, 'Teacher, which is the great commandment in the Law?' " (Matthew 22:35, 36).

To appreciate this question, you need some background. The scribes had attempted to count the laws in the Old Testament. The totals varied. Some said there were 485; others said over 600. But all agreed the total was in the hundreds. This made many of them throw up their hands and say, "Who can ever keep all those laws?!" They then came up with the idea: "Let's divide the law into greater commandments and lesser commandments—and as long as we keep the greater commandments, we are all right." Some had taken the idea a step further: "If we can determine which is the *great* commandment and keep that, it will matter little whether we keep the others or not." The problem was that they could not agree on what that "great" commandment was. Some thought it was sacrifices. Others, the wearing of phylacteries, the commands regarding purification, the Great Feasts, the Sabbath, or the sacredness of human life. One would assume that regardless of what answer Jesus gave, He would disagree with the majority of religious teachers.

Jesus replied, " 'You shall love the Lord your God with all your heart, and with all your soul, and with all your mind.' This is the great and foremost commandment" (Matthew 22:37, 38). In Mark's account, several words are added to the first part of the answer: "The foremost is, 'Hear, O Israel! The Lord our God is one Lord; and you shall. . . .' " (Mark 12:29, 30). Jesus' words were well known to every Jew. They are found in Deuteronomy 6:4-9, found immediately after the second giving of the Ten Commandments:

"Hear, O Israel! The Lord is our God, the Lord is one! And you shall love the Lord your God with all your heart and with all your soul and with all your might. And these words, which I am commanding you today, shall be on your heart; and you shall teach them diligently to your sons and shall talk of them when you sit in your house and when you walk by the way and when you lie down and when you rise up. And you shall bind them as a sign on your hand and they shall be as frontals on your forehead. And you shall write them on the doorposts of your house and on your gates."

These words are called "the Shema," from the first word in the passage (the Hebrew word for "hear") and were used at the beginning of every Jewish service, festival, and ceremony. They were echoed again and again. They were extremely familiar words to every faithful Jew.

For instance, earlier in Jesus' ministry, another lawyer came to Him, also testing Him, who asked Him, "Teacher, what shall I do to inherit eternal life?" (Luke 10:25). Instead of answering, Jesus asked him a question, "What is written in the Law? How does it read to you?" (v. 26). The lawyer had replied, "You shall love the Lord your God with all your heart, and with all your soul, and with all your strength, and with all your mind; and your neighbor as yourself" (v. 27). Jesus said, "You have answered correctly; do this, and you will live" (v. 28).

Returning to Matthew 22, Jesus says that these familiar words were "the great and foremost commandment." They were *great* because the commandment to love God is the foundation of all the law of God and *foremost* because in a sense this commandment takes in all the other commandments of God.

Jesus had answered the lawyer's question fairly, but then He threw in a bonus for them. He had not been asked what the second commandment was, but He told them anyway: "The second is like it, 'You shall love your neighbor as yourself.' On these two commandments depend the whole Law and the Prophets" (vv. 39, 40).

Jesus' "second commandment" also came from an Old Testament passage, Leviticus 19:18: "You shall not take vengeance, nor bear any grudge against the sons of your people, but you shall love your neighbor as yourself; I am the Lord." This passage was more obscure than Deuteronomy 6, but was still well known by those versed in the law, as we saw in Luke 10.

Mark gives a detailed account of the result of Jesus' answer:

> And the scribe said to Him, "Right, Teacher, You have truly stated that He is One; and there is no one else besides Him; and to love Him with all the heart and with all the understanding and with all the strength, and to love one's neighbor as himself, is much more than all burnt offerings and sacrifices." And when Jesus saw that he had answered intelligently, He said to him, "You are not far from the kingdom of God" . . . (Mark 12:32-34).

Jesus' enemies were silenced. Jesus then asked *them* several questions (Matthew 22:41-45). Verse 46 says, "And no one was able to answer Him a word, nor did anyone dare from that day on to ask Him another question." Jesus had won the day.

LOVE'S PRIORITIES

With that by way of background, let us take a closer look at Matthew 22:37-39. Notice again the priorities of love:

(1) *The Lord God* (vv. 37, 38). Jesus says this is number one.

(2) *Your neighbor* (v. 39). Jesus says this is number two. And by implication:

(3) *Yourself* (v. 39). Let me hasten to say this is not commandment number three, although some seem to think that it is. Only two commandments are here, not three. This one is more or less taken for granted, but it is still here, so we place it number three.

Think of a target with concentric circles (a small circle in the middle with larger circles around it). The outside circle is labeled "yourself." Closer to the center is the circle labeled "your neighbor." But the bull's eye is identified as "The Lord God"!

This will not be a new thought to the children who learn the song "J—O—Y":

> J—O—Y, J—O—Y,
> Surely this must mean
> Jesus first and yourself last
> And others in between.

These are not three mutually exclusive loves. Of necessity they overlap. Notice the text: "The second is *like* [the first]" and "love your neighbor *as* yourself" (Matthew 22:39; emphasis mine). Remember the point made in 1 John 4:20, 21:

> If someone says, "I love God," and hates his brother, he is a liar; for the one who does not love his brother whom he has seen, cannot love God

89

whom he has not seen. And this commandment we have from Him, that the one who loves God should love his brother also.

But still Jesus establishes some priorities in Matthew 22:37-39, and that is the thrust of this chapter. Our next chapters will be on numbers two and three in the priority list. The next study will be "Self-Love Vs. Selfishness." A fine line exists between the two, and it is important that we try to find that line. Then we will have several chapters on loving others: our neighbors, our enemies, those we plan to marry, those we do marry, those in the church. But for the remainder of this chapter, I want to stress that the number one priority in our lives is to love *God* with all.

THE FIRST PRIORITY

Loving God with all is the beginning point of our love, the foundation and heart of it all. In 2 Corinthians 5:14, Paul says, "The love of Christ controls us."

It is this that gives meaning and validity to all other expressions of love. Writer and speaker Thomas Warren has a book titled *Marriage Is for Those Who Love God and One Other*. Many studies have shown that the happiest and most enduring marriages are those in which the couples are walking together in their religious life, not only united in heart and body but also in spirit. "Big Don" Williams, who has spent his life working with young people, tells them if they are going to have really enjoyable dates, there always needs to be three on the date: themselves, their date, and God.

The completeness of this love for God is seen in the qualifying phrases used by Jesus. Matthew's account gives a threefold division: One is to love God with all the heart, all the soul, and all the mind. Mark's account really says the same thing, but gives a fourfold division. He mentions the heart, the soul, the mind, and then adds "all your strength."

These express the totality of man.[2] The mind is the thinking part of man, the part with which we reason and make our plans. The heart in this context refers to the emotional part of man. Our love for God is not to be cold and calculating; it has an emotional side. There has to be a blending of head and heart. The strength takes in one's energies—and time and talents. God gave us all these, and we are to dedicate them to Him. The soul can refer to the immortal part of man or to one's life in its entirety. Either way the emphasis is on the whole man. All of our being is to be involved in our love for God.

The key word is the word "all": *all* your heart, soul, mind, and strength. Other loves have qualifications and restrictions, not so with our love for God. It is to be unqualified and unrestricted. As we noted earlier, some of the Jews in Jesus' day wanted to obey one commandment, the "great one," whatever it was. But Jesus says that the great commandment is to give oneself totally to the Lord!

Let it be noted that Matthew 22 emphasizes that love for God is not just a warm feeling toward the Almighty. It is practical. It is expressed in our think-

---

[2]For an excellent lesson on "loving God with all," see Batsell Barrett Baxter's sermon "The Greatest Commandment of All" in *If I Be Lifted Up* (Nashville, Tenn.: Gospel Advocate Co., 1956), 9-18.

ing, our actions, and our every moment. We need also to note that love for God takes in all to which God is related. Love for God would obviously take in our love for Jesus. Love for God includes our love for the church. Jesus loves the church (Ephesians 5:25); so should we. The kingdom/church should be first in our lives (Matthew 6:33).

Further, love for God includes a love for God's Word, the Bible. Second Thessalonians 2:10ff. tells how important it is to have a "love of the truth." And a love of the truth means that we will desire with all our hearts to obey that truth. Several verses need to be indelibly stamped upon our hearts. In John 14:15, Jesus says, "If you love Me, you will keep My commandments." In 1 John 5:3, the apostle stresses, "This is the love of God, that we keep His commandments; and His commandments are not burdensome."

If we can learn the priority of putting God first in our love, it can put many things into perspective.

I love my family, my friends and others, but these can never come before God. Love seeks the best for the ones loved, and the best thing I can do for those I love is be a good example to them, to show them that I truly love the Lord.

For instance, there is the practical matter of church attendance (Hebrews 10:25). If your mate is not a Christian and he/she suggests that you miss a worship service, the response must be, "I love you. I love you more than you will ever know. But I love the Lord more. And He has asked me to be present when the saints meet." This is "seeking the best" for your mate, for he/she will never be won to the Lord by half-hearted service on your part.

If our children want to play ball, go to play rehearsal, or do any number of activities on Wednesday evening instead of coming to midweek service, we must say, "I know that it means a great deal to you to participate and that you want to please your fellow students and your leader, but as your parent it's my responsibility to teach you to put God and His ways first. I love you too much to allow you to put God in second place."

Back in the days before VCR's, Patti Page had her own TV show. Her parents, who were members of the church, were asked if they were proud of their daughter's program. "We don't know," they said, "we've never seen it." The program was telecast on Wednesday evenings.

Or there is the matter of traveling during holidays and at other times. If we really love the Lord, we will find out where God's people meet and be with them at Bible study and worship time.

I think the principle of loving God with all can even affect one's decision about taking a job where he would have to work during service times. Yes, I know that these are hard times financially and that every Christian has to deal with this problem individually and personally. I know that it gets hard when you are the person who is responsible for supporting your family. But I get very concerned about what we are teaching our children. I see more and more young people, when they are old enough to get a job, show little or no concern about whether their job will affect their attendance or not. These young people are *not* working to support a family. Many or most are working for spending money, gas money, or money to pay for a car.

Am I being too hard? Am I asking too much? I do not

93

think so, not if we understand how God has—and does—love us!

CONCLUSION

Priorities. What a big word that is. What a challenge to get our priorities straight! How can I meet this challenge? Put God *first*, and then let *Him* put numbers on everything else. Please keep this in mind as we approach the next chapters. Whether stated or not, this will always be the perspective from which we are proceeding.

Class Discussion and Activity

1. Make a chart on a piece of paper with nine lines and as many columns as you have translations. On the lefthand side, list the nine qualities of love as given in 1 Corinthians 13:4-7. At the top of each column put the name of a translation. Then beside each quality, put how each translation expresses that quality. This can give you a "feel" for each quality that can be gained in no other way. (You may want to do this together in class on the chalkboard.)

2. "Patient": Are there some people with whom you have a hard time being patient? Share ideas for developing more patience.

3. "Kind": Is it true that we are often the most unkind to those we are the closest to? Share some practical ways to show kindness.

4. "Not jealous": Have you ever been jealous of someone else's success? Share ideas on how to

deal with jealousy.

5. "Humble": In the last paragraph in the section "The Problem of Pride: Love Is Humble," underline the sentence that begins, "If I understand the biblical concept of humility, . . ." Do you agree or disagree with this statement?

6. "Courteous": Do you think people are as courteous as they once were? How can we teach our children to be courteous?

7. "Unselfish": Is it hard to be unselfish? Share ideas on how to start thinking more about others.

8. "Good-natured": Can we *learn* not to be quick-tempered? Share some ideas on how to do this?

9. "Believes the best": Be honest. Have you ever held a grudge? How can we overcome this tendency?

10. "Concerned": Are we as concerned as we should be about sin in the lives of others? How can we overcome our indifference?

11. A suggestion: Pick out *one* of the qualities of love that you think is lacking in your life, and *consciously* work on it this coming week. (If the members of your class are close, this could be a class project with each sharing next week how he or she did.)

7
Self-Love Vs. Selfishness

Before my family and I left for Australia the first of 1968, passages like these were stressed in pulpits all over the land:

> All of us like sheep have gone astray, each of us has turned to his own way (Isaiah 53:6).

> . . . all our righteous deeds are like a filthy garment; . . . (Isaiah 64:6).

> . . . "There is none righteous, not even one;" (Romans 3:10).

> For all have sinned and fall short of the glory of God (Romans 3:23).

It was noted that Jesus said, "Blessed are the poor in spirit, for theirs is the kingdom of heaven" (Matthew 5:3) and that the Greek word translated "poor" does not mean having little, but having nothing. The picture is that of a man, realizing his spiritual destitution, extending an empty hand to God. The phrase "self-esteem" was not unknown at the time we left the U.S., but certainly it was not a major theological consideration.

When we returned to America the latter part of 1977, the religious atmosphere was saturated with the concept of self-esteem, with a key word being "self-image." Books, sermons, articles, posters declared that mankind has a self-image problem and that, if we will all develop a good self-image, most, if not all, of our problems will disappear. Christian parents were being told that the greatest challenge they faced was to develop a good self-image in their children.

I am not too proud to admit that it is always possible that I have missed something in the Bible. If the Bible has that much to say about a subject, I certainly want to preach it. So I attempted an in-depth study of the subject of self-esteem. I discovered that although a variety of passages are used to prove that man, especially Christians, should have a good self-image, invariably the starting point was one of the main texts we have been studying: ". . . 'You shall love your neighbor as yourself' " (Matthew 22:39), with emphasis on the words "as yourself."

As far as I know, no one denies the fact that Jesus (and others) implied a love for self in Matthew 22:39 and other passages that quote Leviticus 19:18. But was Jesus teaching what some today say He was teaching? What *does* it mean to love oneself?

This will not primarily be a lesson on self-esteem. No doubt many are crippled in their personal and religious lives because they have a very poor self-image. This was emphasized in a recent meeting with a group of preachers. One preacher told of members who had never known the joy of Christianity. Many preachers spoke of trying to help people who are destroying their marriages and other relationships basically because they do not like themselves. On Monday nights I meet with a divorce recovery group, and one of the things many of those present struggle with is the matter of restoring self-respect.

There is no way that I can cover all that could be and should be discussed on this topic. My purpose will be to discuss what it means to love oneself and the subject of self-esteem only indirectly, as it relates to our text. Hopefully, however, some things will be said that will be helpful to those struggling with low self-esteem.

My approach will be a series of five contrasts. In each case I will first discuss what love of self does *not* mean biblically and then what it *does* mean.

LOVE OF SELF DOES *NOT* MEAN JESUS GAVE A THIRD COMMANDMENT

Some leave the impression that Jesus gave three commandments in Matthew 22:37-40: (1) Love God; (2) love your neighbor; (3) love yourself. But our text stresses that Jesus gave only two commandments: "This is *the* great and foremost commandment. The *second* is like it, . . . On these *two* commandments depend the whole Law and the Prophets." (Emphasis mine.) I mention this because some seem to believe that if an individual does not feel good about himself, he is guilty of disobeying a basic principle of the Lord. Thus some are sent on a guilt trip because they do *not* "feel good" about themselves.

LOVE OF SELF *DOES* MEAN
SELF-LOVE IS NATURAL

Rather than command us to love ourselves, our text *assumes* that we love ourselves. Self-love is considered to be axiomatic, self-evident. Most of us normally take care of ourselves; that is the way God has put us together. An old English proverb says, "Self-preservation is the first law of nature." On the other hand, we are not so constituted that we automatically love *others*. So Jesus says we should love others *as* we love ourselves.

LOVE OF SELF DOES *NOT* MEAN
WE MUST "FEEL GOOD" ABOUT OURSELVES

The word for "love" in Matthew 22:37-40 is a form of *agape*. Remember what has been said about *agape* love: *Agape* is not *devoid* of emotion, but it is not *dependent* upon emotion. When we *agapao* our enemies, we are not required to have warm feelings toward them. As I type this in a motel room, my wife is watching a TV program about rapists. I doubt seriously that a woman who is raped, even a Christian woman, is commanded to "feel good" about the rapist. She is commanded to love this man, to care for his soul, but she does not have to have warm feelings toward him. "Feeling good" is not an inherent part of *agape* love.

There *is* a passage that speaks of self-love in the sense of feeling good about oneself: 2 Timothy 3:1-5. In verse 2, "lovers of self" is from *philia* (love) and *autos* (self). Remember that *philia* involves warm feelings and emotions. Think about what Paul is saying; here are the by-products of the wrong kind of self-love:

> But realize this, that in the last days difficult
> times will come. For men will be *lovers of self*,
> lovers of money, boastful, arrogant, revilers, dis-
> obedient to parents, ungrateful, unholy, unlov-
> ing, irreconcilable, malicious gossips, without
> self-control, brutal, haters of good, treacherous,
> reckless, conceited, lovers of pleasure rather
> than lovers of God. (Emphasis mine.)

Do not misunderstand me. I am not saying that a
Christian is required to feel bad about himself all the
time. At times we *should* feel bad about ourselves,
specifically when we are confronted with our sins.
This is called "guilt," and in God's arrangement, guilt
is designed to make us repent of our sins and turn to
Him so we can be forgiven by His grace. If we never
feel bad about ourselves, something is terribly wrong
with our consciences. On the other hand, there are
certainly many reasons for a Christian to feel good
about himself. For example, there is the teaching of
Jesus, the life of Jesus, and the death of Jesus.

Jesus taught that God made you (Matthew 19:4),
and, as has been often noted, "God don't make no
junk." Jesus also taught that you are worth more than
all the world: "For what will a man be profited, if he
gains the whole world, and forfeits his soul? Or what
will a man give in exchange for his soul?" (Matthew
16:26). And there is the life of Jesus; He left heaven
and came to this world for *you*:

> Have this attitude in yourselves which was also
> in Christ Jesus, who, although He existed in the
> form of God, did not regard equality with God a
> thing to be grasped, but emptied Himself, taking
> the form of a bond-servant, and being made in

the likeness of men. And being found in appearance as a man, He humbled Himself by becoming obedient to the point of death, even death on a cross (Philippians 2:5-8).

And never forget the death of Jesus; He loves you and died for you (John 3:16). If there had been no one else on earth except you, Jesus would still have died for you.

I am not saying that you should feel bad about yourself. I *am* saying that "feeling good about self" is not under consideration in Matthew 22:39.

LOVE OF SELF *DOES* MEAN
WE SHOULD TAKE CARE OF OURSELVES

The basic meaning of *agape* love is to "seek the best for" the ones loved, to take care of needs. In Ephesians 5:28, 29, Paul gave what is probably the best explanation of what it means to "love self": "So husbands ought also to love their own wives *as their own bodies*. He who loves his own wife *loves himself;* for no one ever hated his own flesh, but *nourishes and cherishes it, . . .*" (Emphasis mine.) "Loving self" involves at least three "p's": (1) provision, (2) protection, and (3) preservation—in other words, taking care of one's needs.

Perhaps it should be noted in passing that in addition to physical needs, each of us also has emotional needs. We need security: physical security for the future and emotional security (unconditional acceptance). We also need to feel that we have value. To fulfill this need, we must have a purpose in life and the opportunity to develop our full potential. Since love for self means that we take care of ourselves and supply our needs, within reason one can legitimately try to supply these emotional needs. But note this warning: If the fulfillment of these needs becomes a major aim in our lives, our efforts will be self-defeating. As author James Dobson notes: "Unlike the appetite for food, water, sex, and other physiological requirements of the body, the need for self-esteem becomes more demanding as it is gratified."[1]

LOVE OF SELF DOES *NOT* MEAN
A GOOD SELF-IMAGE IS ALL-IMPORTANT

I certainly would not claim that a good self-image is unimportant. A good self-image can help us in many pursuits of this life. Think of the athlete who "psyches himself up" before the big contest. Also a good self-image can help in our relationships with others, or a poor self-image can hurt those relationships. If I cannot get along with myself, I probably will not be able to get along with others. But it is still true that nothing is in our text, nor in any other passage in the Bible that I am aware of, that suggests that developing a good self-image should be a major pursuit in life.

In fact, as we go through the Bible, we find many godly individuals who had what would today be termed "poor self-images," especially as they came face to face with their sinfulness and/or the glory of God. Consider, for instance, David's statement in Psalms 22:6: "I am a worm and no man," or Job's statement in Job 42:6: "I abhor myself" (KJV). Yet these individuals still led productive lives in the Lord.

---

[1]James Dobson, *Hide or Seek* (Old Tappan, N.J.: Fleming H. Revell Co., 1979), 170.

LOVE OF SELF *DOES* MEAN
WE CAN HAVE A POOR SELF-IMAGE
AND STILL PLEASE GOD

According to our text, Matthew 22:39, if we (1) love God and (2) love others, we will please God.

We need to understand that it is possible to have a good self-image and still be lost. In Luke 18, Jesus tells of a Pharisee who went to the temple to pray. It is obvious from his words that he had a great self-image: "God, I thank Thee that I am not like other people: swindlers, unjust, adulterers, . . . I fast twice a week; I pay tithes of all that I get" (vv. 11, 12). But his prayer was not heard.

On the other hand, it is possible to have a poor self-image and be saved. This point is made by John:

> We shall know by this that we are of the truth, and shall assure our heart before Him, in whatever our heart condemns us; for God is greater than our heart, and knows all things. Beloved, if our heart does not condemn us, we have confidence before God (1 John 3:19-21).

Two types of individuals are depicted by John. Both of these are godly individuals. Both have accepted Jesus as divine, and both are obeying God. But one still has a heart that condemns him, in other words a guilty conscience. Maybe it is because of the way he was reared. He never believes that he deserves forgiveness. He does not know the joy of salvation. But the other individual has a heart that does not condemn him; he has a clear conscience. As a result, he has great confidence in his Christian life. It is obvious that John wants us all to be like the second individual. We should try our hardest to believe the promises of God. Among other things, we need to learn to forgive ourselves.

But you can be like the *first* individual and still be saved. As long as we are Christians and are striving with all our might to do what God wants us to do, even if our heart still condemns us, we can take comfort in this great truth: "God is greater than our heart"!

The two types of individuals might be compared with two people who board an airplane. One is terrified of flying and never relaxes the entire flight. The other has no fear at all and enjoys the flight. *But both make it to the destination.*

Do not misunderstand me. God wants us to enjoy the Christian journey; He does not want us to be terrified the entire trip. Each of us needs to be building our faith and confidence in the Lord so that the Christian life grows sweeter each day that we live. But if, by reason of temperament or upbringing, we never learn to relax totally in our Christianity, this need not be fatal. As long as we do not let our concern about our spiritual condition discourage us to the point that we quit, we can have what the world calls a poor self-image and still be saved.

LOVE OF SELF DOES *NOT* MEAN
WE SHOULD "MAJOR" IN SELF

We live today in the "me" generation. First, we had a magazine called *Life*. Then *People* magazine began to be published. Then there was a magazine called *Us*, followed by one called *Self*. It has been suggested that if the trend continues we will finally have one called *Me*, filled with pages of aluminum foil, so I can look at *me*. The following limerick expresses the self-centered attitude of today:

> There once was a nymph named Narcissus,
> Who thought himself very delicious;
> So he stared like a fool
> At his face in a pool,
> And his folly today is still with us.

As I reflect on the self-centeredness of today, I wonder if much of what we are hearing on self-esteem is not more a reflection of this age than it is a reflection of the clear-cut teaching of the Bible.

If anything is taught in the Scriptures, it is the danger of putting too much stress on self. The rich man in Luke 12 was concerned solely with self:

> "And he began reasoning to himself, saying, 'What shall *I* do, since *I* have no place to store *my* crops?' And he said, 'This is what *I* will do: *I* will tear down *my* barns and build larger ones, and there *I* will store all *my* grain and *my* goods. And *I* will say to *my* soul, "Soul, you have many goods laid up for many years to come; take your ease, eat, drink, and be merry"'" (vv. 17-19; emphasis mine).

God said to this selfish man: "You fool! This very night your soul is required of you; and now who will own what you have prepared?" (v. 20). Jesus said, "So is the man who lays up treasure for *himself*, and is not rich toward God" (v. 21; emphasis mine).

Throughout the Bible, it is stressed that the heart of sin is selfishness.

If you would like to study the relationship of self-love and selfishness in depth, I would recommend the book *The Danger of Self-Love* by Paul Brownback. He notes that "for almost two thousand years theologians studied Scripture without discovering the doctrine of self-love as we now have it."[2] He further notes that the first contemporary writer to use the verses on loving self to teach that self-love is a matter of great significance was not a religious writer, but a self-confessed humanist by the name of Erich Fromm.[3]

It is an extremely dangerous thing spiritually to "major" in self, whatever the motivation.

LOVE OF SELF *DOES* MEAN WE SHOULD "MINOR" IN SELF

Rather than teach us that we should "major" in self, our text declares that we should "minor" in self. As we saw in our chapter on the priorities of love, self is to come after God and our neighbor. In our next chapter we will see that the term "neighbor" actually takes in anyone—and we would not be out of place to say, everyone. Since the world population passed the five billion mark late in 1986 or early in 1987, today it would be well over that figure. For our purposes, though, let us say that it is still about five billion. If God is to be first, everyone else next, and myself last, that puts me about five-billionth! Any way you look at it, that is "way down the list"! There is no encouragement in our text to exalt self, and there is every encouragement to depreciate self.

The Scriptures do not emphasize self-love. Neither

---

[2]Paul Brownback, *The Danger of Self-Love* (Chicago, Ill.: Moody Press, 1982), 69.
[3]Ibid., 51.

GETTING SERIOUS ABOUT LOVE

do they teach self-hatred. What they do teach is *self-forgetfulness*. Take some time to think about these passages and the implications of them:

> Then Jesus said to His disciples, "If anyone wishes to come after Me, *let him deny himself*, and take up his cross, and follow Me. For whoever wishes to save his life shall lose it; but whoever loses his life for My sake shall find it" (Matthew 16:24-26; emphasis mine).

> "Thus the last shall be first, and the first last" (Matthew 20:16).

> "Whoever exalts himself shall be humbled; and whoever humbles himself shall be exalted" (Matthew 23:12).

> . . . I say to every man among you not to think more highly of himself than he ought to think; . . . (Romans 12:3).

> Let no one seek his own good, but that of his neighbor (1 Corinthians 10:24).

> . . . love does not brag and is not arrogant, does not act unbecomingly; it does not seek its own, . . . (1 Corinthians 13:4, 5).

Jesus did not say, "I'll meet you at the top," but rather, "I'll meet you at the bottom—as you learn to serve." Self-acceptance is good, but self-forgetfulness is better—and self-sacrifice is best.

The emphasis in the Scriptures is not on *self*-esteem, but on *other*-esteem.

> Do nothing from selfishness or empty conceit, but with humility of mind let each of you regard [or esteem] one another as more important than himself (Philippians 2:3).

. . . appreciate those who diligently labor among you, . . . and . . . esteem them very highly in love because of their work. . . . (1 Thessalonians 5:12, 13).

A feeling of self-worth is much like a feeling of happiness or contentment; if any of these is pursued as an end within itself, it is elusive. But often, if we will forget self and concentrate on making others feel good or happy or contented, a by-product is that these feelings become our own.

LOVE OF SELF DOES *NOT* MEAN THIS LOVE IS DEPENDENT UPON THE WORLD'S STANDARDS

Some time ago I bought James Dobson's book *Hide or Seek*, which has the subtitle: *How to Build Self-Esteem in Your Child.* I love the book and recommend it to every parent. The main thrust of the book is that the reason so many of us are struggling with the problem of self-esteem is because we have bought into this world's value system. He speaks of beauty as the golden coin of human worth and of intelligence as the silver coin of human worth, followed closely by the coin of money. He notes that from birth we are programmed to believe that we have little value unless we have these qualities that the world considers to be valuable. Even our fairy tales proclaim this message. Would the Prince have kissed Sleeping Ugly?

But our value is not dependent upon such superficial things. The devil has sold us a bill of goods. We enjoy being attractive, intelligent, popular, successful—but all such things are transient—here and then gone. "The world is passing away, and also its lusts; but the one who does the will of God abides forever" (1 John 2:17).

If I buy into the world's value system, not only will it make me not like myself, but also I will dislike other people. If I cannot love myself unless I am pretty, smart, or successful, neither will I be able to love others unless they are attractive, intelligent, or financially successful. It is so hard not to accept the world's evaluation of worth, but if I am to be a Christian who really loves others, I must strive to reject such superficial criteria.

LOVE OF SELF *DOES* MEAN
TO REALLY LOVE OURSELVES;
OUR ATTENTION MUST BE FOCUSED ON GOD

The more some of us work on having a better self-image, the less self-esteem we will have. The closer we look at ourselves, the more aware we are of our shortcomings, and no amount of rationalization will convince us that we are really super-special people. When the great prophet Elijah took his eyes off of God and looked closely at himself, he went to the depths of despair: ". . . now, O Lord, take my life, for I am not better than my fathers. . . . I alone am left; and they seek my life, to take it away" (1 Kings 19:4, 10). We need to get our minds off ourselves and ourselves off our minds. Self-examination followed by repentance and a change of life is always of value (2 Corinthians 13:5; 7:10). On the other hand, an excessive amount of spiritual navel-gazing is an exercise in self-indulgence and seldom results in anything of value.

Our text, Matthew 22:39, declares that what *is* important is a right relationship with *God*. When you have that, He will supply all your needs, including your emotional needs. As Paul emphasized:

> And my God shall supply all your needs according to His riches in glory in Christ Jesus (Philippians 4:19).

> Now to Him who is able to do exceeding abundantly beyond all that we ask or think, according to the power that works within us, to Him be the glory in the church and in Christ Jesus to all generations forever and ever. Amen (Ephesians 3:20, 21).

I earlier noted basic physical and emotional needs that all of us have. It is important for the Christian to realize that all of these are met in Jesus Christ. Our basic physical needs are supplied if we "seek first" the kingdom of God (Matthew 6:33). Our need for physical security for the future is met as we have the assurance that God will be with us and give us what we need (Matthew 6:34; Philippians 4:6). Our need for emotional security, unconditional acceptance, is met in Christ; God's love is unconditional (Romans 5:8; 8:35, 39). The need to have a purpose in life so we can feel worthwhile and significant is supplied in the Lord; He gives us purpose for this life and the hope for the one to come (Philippians 1:21; Ephesians 2:10). And the need for what some psychologists call "self-actualization," or the opportunity to develop one's full potential, is fulfilled in Christianity as we have the opportunity and challenge to grow up into Christ, to become spiritually mature (Ephesians 4:15; Colossians 1:28; etc.).

In Dobson's book on building self-esteem in our children, after he has spent pages giving many valuable suggestions, he gets to the bottom line:

> The most valuable contribution a parent can make to his child is to instill in him a genuine faith in God. What greater ego satisfaction could there be than knowing that the Creator of the Universe is acquainted with me, personally? That He values me more than the possessions of the entire world; that He understands my fears and my anxieties; that He reaches out to me in immeasurable love when no one else cares; that His only Son actually gave His life for me; that He can turn my liabilities into assets and my emptiness into fullness; that a better life follows this one, where the present handicaps and inadequacies will all be eliminated—where earthly pain and suffering will be no more than a dim memory! What a beautiful philosophy with which to "clothe" your tender child. What a fantastic message of hope and encouragement for the broken teen-ager who has been crushed by life's circumstances. This is self-esteem at its richest, not dependent on the whims of birth or social judgment, or the cult of the superchild, but on divine decree.[4]

If for some reason you do not like yourself, I do not blame you for trying everything you can to restore some measure of self-respect. But most of the cures for poor self-esteem as proposed by men are little more than psychological Band-aids. The only real cure comes in a close relationship with God. Most of us need to look less at self and more at God.

As in all other matters, we need a balance. The

---

[4]Dobson, 169-70.

Christian who has learned to look to God does not say, "I'm wonderful," but neither does he say, "I'm worthless." Rather he says, "I have a wonderful *Lord*—and I can do all things through Him (Philippians 4:13)! I am a sinner, but God loved me anyway. Praise His name! Now I depend on Him!"

Class Discussion and Activity

1. Have we developed a "self-image cult" in America? What are the dangers in this?
2. On the other hand, do some (even Christians) suffer from a lack of self-respect? Why do you suppose this is so? Give some reasons a *Christian* should have a healthy self-respect.
3. When Matthew 22:37-40 implies we will love ourselves, the word for "love" is *agapao*. Is *agape* love primarily a "feel-good-about" love? We are to *agapao* our enemies (Matthew 5:44). Does this mean we must have a warm feeling toward them? Are we, therefore, *commanded* to "feel good about" ourselves?
4. What are the three "p's" involved in loving self? Discuss what each includes.
5. James Dobson stated, ". . . the need for self-esteem becomes more demanding as it is gratified." Do you agree?
6. The author suggests we can have what the world would call a "poor self-image" and still be saved. In this connection, read and study 1 John 3:19-21 in context.
7. Optional: Have someone read Paul Brownback's book *The Danger of Self-Love* and report on it.

8. In class, put the following words on the chalk-board, and discuss how each relates to the Christian (and which are the more important for the Christian): self-hatred, self-love, self-acceptance, self-forgetfulness, self-sacrifice.
9. Optional: Have someone read James Dobson's book *Hide or Seek* and report on it. (You may want to get a copy or two and put it in the church library and encourage your parents to read.)
10. All men have certain basic needs. Among them are: basic physical needs (such as food and air), physical security, emotional security, a purpose in life, the opportunity to develop one's potential. Discuss how all of these are met in Christ.

8
Love Put to the Test

Make no mistake about it, we live in a crazy, mixed-up world. We can put a man on the moon, but we cannot get along with our next-door neighbor. We invent methods of prolonging life and then invent methods of killing off half the population of the earth. We have more things than we have ever had before, but we are afraid to go out by ourselves at night.

More and more authorities are realizing that if we do not learn to get along—to *love* each other—civilization as we know it is doomed. Ordway Tead put it this way in the *Illinois Medical Journal*:

> More and more clearly every day out of biology, anthropology, sociology, history, economic analysis, psychological insight, plain human decency, and common sense, the necessary mandate of survival that we show love of our neighbors as we do ourselves, is being confirmed and reaffirmed.[1]

[1]Frank S. Mean, ed. and comp., *The Encyclopedia of Religious Quotations* (Westwood, N.J.: Fleming H. Revell Co., 1965), 286.

Even Bertrand Russell, author of *Why I Am Not a Christian* and representative atheist-humanist, had to admit this:

> The root of the matter is a very simple and old fashioned thing, so simple that I am almost ashamed to mention it for fear of the derisive smile with which the cynics will greet my words.— The thing I mean—please pardon me for mentioning it—is love—Christian love or compassion.[2]

As a popular song said a few years ago, "What the world needs now is love, sweet love."

That need was confirmed by Jesus almost two thousand years ago. A lawyer came to Jesus testing Him with the question: "Which is the great commandment in the Law?" (Matthew 22:36). Jesus replied:

> "You shall love the Lord your God with all your heart, and with all your soul, and all your mind." This is the great and foremost commandment. The second is like it, "You shall love your neighbor as yourself." On these two commandments depend the whole Law and the Prophets (Matthew 22:37-40).

In a previous chapter, we briefly discussed this text and stressed commandment number one: loving God. In a subsequent chapter, we struggled with the concept of loving self. In this chapter we want to discuss the concept of loving our neighbors as ourselves.

---

[2]Quoted in *Voices of Concern* (Austin, Tex.: R. B. Sweet Co., 1968), 143-44.

LOVE PUT TO THE TEST: "YOU SHALL LOVE YOUR NEIGHBOR AS YOURSELF"

The commandment "Love your neighbor as yourself" was first given by Moses (Leviticus 19:18) and then repeated by Jesus and other inspired speakers and writers in the New Testament. Its importance cannot be overemphasized. The commandment, given in these words, is found eight times in the New Testament.

Learning to love our neighbor is inescapably linked to our love for God.

> If some one says, "I love God," and hates his brother, he is a liar; for the one who does not love his brother whom he has seen, cannot love God whom he has not seen. And this commandment we have from Him, that the one who loves God should love his brother also (1 John 4:20, 21).

Thus we have passages like those that follow.

When Jesus was answering the rich young ruler's question on what he had to do to inherit eternal life, part of His answer was in these words: "You shall love your neighbor as yourself" (Matthew 19:19).

When Paul wrote the Galatians concerning their treatment of each other, he said: "For the whole Law is fulfilled in one word, in the statement, 'You shall love your neighbor as yourself' " (Galatians 5:14).

When James wrote against showing partiality, this verse is in the heart of his discussion: "If . . . you are fulfilling the royal law, according to the Scripture, 'You shall love your neighbor as yourself,' you are doing well" (James 2:8).

117

This is where love is put to the test—as I am challenged to open my heart enough to love people and to get along with others. This is a test for *all* of us.

It is a test for those that are younger. Every poll I have seen of needs expressed by teen-agers has this near the top of the list: How to get along with others.

It is a test for those of us who are older. We are set in our ways. We have the prejudices of a lifetime. We have our little schedules all worked out and our little circle of friends with whom we feel comfortable. To break the mold is so hard.

Someone has said that any preacher who says that this is an easy command proves one of two things: (1) He has never tried it, or (2) he has awfully nice neighbors. Consider this little poem:

> To love the whole world
> For me is no chore;
> My only real problem's
> The neighbor next door.

THE TEST OF LOVING ALL MEN: "YOUR NEIGHBOR"

To appreciate this test, let us break down the command into three parts. First, let us take the phrase "your neighbor." Who is the "neighbor" who is mentioned in the command? Probably the best answer is found in Luke 10:25-37. Another lawyer attempted to put Jesus to the test by asking Him, "Teacher, what shall I do to inherit eternal life?" Instead of answering, Jesus asked the lawyer a question: "What is written in the Law? How does it read to you?" He answered, "You shall love the Lord your God with all your heart, and with all your soul, and with all your strength, and with all your mind; and your neighbor as yourself." Jesus said, "You have answered correctly; do this, and you will live."

One can imagine the lawyer wondering what hit him. Instead of Jesus' being embarrassed, it was he, the expert in the law, who had been put on the spot. So he blurted out the question, "And who is my neighbor?" This was another controversial question, one on which the specialists in the law of Moses were divided. The English word "neighbor" literally refers to a "near-by-er"—or, as we use the word, the folks who live next door. But Jesus wanted this man—and us—to know that the word means much more. So, by way of reply, He gave the familiar parable of the Good Samaritan (Luke 10:30-37).

> A certain man was going down from Jerusalem to Jericho; and he fell among robbers, and they stripped him and beat him, and went off leaving him half dead. And by chance a certain priest was going down on that road, and when he saw him, he passed by on the other side. And likewise a Levite also, when he came to the place and saw him, passed by on the other side. But a certain Samaritan, who was on a journey, came upon him; . . . (vv. 30-33).

Make no mistake, the Samaritan's love was severely put to the test. In fact, his love was put to a series of tests. There was the *prejudice* test. The Jews and Samaritans were enemies. They hated each other. There was the *priorities* test. No doubt the Samaritan was as busy as the priest and Levite. He had to alter his schedule to stop. There was the *pocketbook* test. Helping not only cost time; it also cost money. But his love passed the tests—as we see in the rest of the story.

> . . . and when he saw him, he felt compassion, and
> came to him, and bandaged up his wounds, pour-
> ing oil and wine on them; and he put him on his
> own beast, and brought him to an inn, and took
> care of him. And on the next day he took out two
> denarii and gave them to the innkeeper and said,
> "Take care of him; and whatever more you
> spend, when I return, I will repay you" (vv.
> 33-35).

Jesus then asked, "Which of these three do you
think proved to be a neighbor to the man who fell into
the robbers' hands?" The lawyer replied, "The one
who showed mercy toward him." Then Jesus said, "Go
and do the same" (v. 37).

The point is that the "neighbor" in the command,
"Love your neighbor," can be *anyone*—specifically
anyone with whom we come in contact who has *needs*
(Galatians 6:10). But since everyone has needs of
some kind—if not physical, then spiritual and perhaps
emotional—the word "anyone" is appropriate. Note
Romans 13:8-10:

> Owe nothing to anyone except to love one
> another; for he who loves his neighbor has ful-
> filled the law. For this, "You shall not commit
> adultery, You shall not murder, You shall not
> steal, You shall not covet," and if there is any
> other commandment, it is summed up in this
> saying, "You shall love your neighbor as your-
> self." Love does no wrong to a neighbor; love
> therefore is the fulfillment of the law.

Notice that Paul says that love is a debt we owe to all
men. Why? Because we are all brothers in the flesh, if
not in the spirit. Because God loved us and we ought

to love others.

Other passages that refer to the command to love our neighbor stress the same thing—that the term "neighbor" takes in all men. In Galatians 5:13-15, the command is applied to how we treat our brethren in Christ. James 2:8 lets me know that my neighbor is the man in ragged clothing who comes to the worship service.

Probably the greatest challenge of this command, however, is given in the Sermon on the Mount. Jesus was contrasting the old law—and the traditions that had come to accompany it—with His new way. Then He came to this contrast:

> You have heard that it was said, "You shall love your neighbor, and hate your enemy." But I say to you, love your enemies, and pray for them who persecute you in order that you may be sons of your Father who is in heaven; for He causes His sun to rise on the evil and the good, and sends rain on the righteous and the unrighteous. For if you love those who love you, what reward have you? Do not even the tax-gatherers do the same? And if you greet your brothers only, what do you do more than others? Do not even the Gentiles do the same? Therefore you are to be perfect, as your heavenly Father is perfect (Matthew 5:43-48).

It is obvious that the Jews of Jesus' day did not understand that a neighbor was anyone with needs—because enemies have needs too. The challenge to us is to be perfect like God—perfect in the sense that our love encompasses both our friends and our enemies as God's love does.

THE TEST OF LOVING THE UNLOVABLE: "YOUR NEIGHBOR" INCLUDES YOUR ENEMY

The challenge to love our enemies is one of the greatest marks of Christianity—and probably the hardest test we will ever have as Christians.

Violate a Muslim, and he will cut off your head in the name of Mohammed. Talk about some eastern dignitary, and he will put you before the firing squad. That is more or less the natural response. The German poet Heinrich Heine gave his description of real happiness:

> My wishes are a humble dwelling with a thatched roof, a good bed, good food, flowers at my windows, and some fine, tall trees, before my door. And if the good God wants really to make me completely happy He will grant me the joy of seeing six or seven of my enemies hanging from the tall, fine trees.[3]

Once a preacher was preaching on loving one's enemies when he stopped to say, "After all, we all have enemies." An old man piped up, "I don't." "That's marvelous!" exclaimed the preacher. "How did that happen?" "I outlived all them rascals," cackled the old man.

I say again that this is the natural reaction. But Jesus says that a Christian is to react differently. Insult a man of the world, and he will hit you. But insult a Christian, and he will pray for you and bring you a bowl of soup when you are sick!

But someone objects, "That's not natural!" Of course it is not. That is the point. Christianity enables

---

[3]Ibid., 152-53.

us to rise above that which is simply natural and fleshly. Peter says that through the promises of God, "you might become partakers of the *divine* nature" (2 Peter 1:4; emphasis mine).

Have you ever thought about the fact that *God's* love was also put to the test? The real test of God's love was not whether He could love folks like Abraham, Joseph, and David. The real test of God's love was whether He could love those like Saul of Tarsus, who was running around like a mad man trying to destroy His church and killing people and breaking up families. It was whether He could love you and me. But, thank God, His love met the test. Now Peter says that with God's help, *we* can be partakers of the *divine* nature. We can learn to love all men, even our enemies.

THE TEST OF *AGAPE* LOVE: "YOU SHALL LOVE"

Let us back up to the first part of the command: "You shall love...." We need to review what this word "love" means. When we are told to love our enemies, the word is *agapao*, which is not so much a matter of the emotion as it is a matter of the will. Our working definition of *agape* love is that which "seeks the best for the one loved." The command is not to *phileo* everyone or to *phileo* our enemies, but to *agapao* them. We are not told we have to *like* everyone, but rather we are told that we are to *love* them. The emphasis regarding this *agape* love is on *helping* people, taking time for them, being concerned enough to meet needs. Paul tells what love *does not* do in Romans 13: "... if there is any other commandment, it is summed up in this saying, 'You shall love your neighbor as yourself.' *Love does no wrong to a neighbor*; love therefore is the fulfillment of the law (vv. 9, 10; emphasis mine). Negatively, if you love your enemy, you will not do anything that will harm him. For the positive aspect, we return to Matthew 5. In verse 44 is a type of Hebrew parallelism. Loving our enemies means that we will pray for them:

> "But I say to you,
>   *love* your enemies,
>   and *pray* for those who persecute you."

Then note Romans 12:19-21 which gives both the negative and positive aspects of loving an enemy:

> Never take your own revenge, beloved, but leave room for the wrath of God, for it is written, "Vengeance is Mine, I will repay," says the Lord. "But if your enemy is hungry, feed him, and if he is thirsty, give him a drink; for in so doing you will heap burning coals upon his head." Do not be overcome by evil, but overcome evil with good.

Negatively, loving an enemy means that you will *not* take revenge. Positively, loving an enemy means that you *will* take care of his needs. In so acting, you will "heap burning coals upon his head"; his conscience may be stirred as he sees you returning good for evil.

Some time ago *Reader's Digest* had an article entitled "Love Your Enemies—It'll Drive 'Em Crazy"—a humorous approach to Romans 12 and Matthew 5. Among other things, the author, J. P. McEvoy, told of a man who bought a farm. When he was looking over his purchase, he met his new neighbor.

"Don't look now," said the neighbor, "but when you bought this piece of ground, you also bought a lawsuit with me. Your fence is three meters over on my land."

The new owner smiled: "I thought I'd find some friendly neighbors here, and I'm going to. And you're going to help me. Move the fence where you want it, and send me the bill. You'll be satisfied and I'll be happy."

The story goes that the fence was never moved, and the potential enemy was never the same. He went around talking to himself. He was in shock; after that he was a slightly mystified but friendly neighbor.

Other passages also stress that the main thrust of how to *agapao* another is to help him. Galatians 5:13, 14 says that the key to loving others is learning to be a servant. In James 2:8ff., loving another means that I will go out of my way to make a poor visitor feel welcome. First Corinthians 13:4-7 summarizes what is involved in my loving all men:

I will be patient with them.

I will be kind to them.

I will not be jealous of them.

I will not be proud and boastful.

I will be courteous to all men.

I will be unselfish in my dealings with others.

I will not wear my feelings on my sleeves.

I will always put the best possible construction on what others do.

I will never be happy when ill befalls another, even an enemy.

I will be able to take anything.

I will believe the best; I will look for the good in people.

I will hope for the best.

I will endure.

In short, in my dealings with others, including my enemies, I will not *react*, but rather *act*—act with love, act as God wants me to act.

Let me back up a little. Regarding the test of loving an enemy, I have stressed that the emphasis is not on liking, but on loving. I have stressed that the emphasis is on serving, helping, and meeting needs. Now let me stress once more that we do not want to toss proper emotions out the window, even in the matter of loving an enemy.

If we are not careful, we can leave the impression that all that is involved in loving an enemy is doing acts. We may give a bowl of soup to a sick enemy with the attitude, "I hope the old so-and-so chokes on it." We may do our acts of concern as we would throw a moldy bone to a snarling dog, just because we are afraid the SPCA will get us otherwise. No, no, no. Love, even *agape* love, can never be thought of as unemotional. Did you notice Luke 10:33? As Jesus described what is involved in loving a neighbor, He said: "And when he [the Samaritan] saw him [the wounded Jew], *he felt compassion*." (Emphasis mine.) The help the Good Samaritan gave to his enemy was not a cold and calculating act; it was a compassionate one.

As we learn to serve, as we learn to help others, as we learn to do good to our enemies, let us also work on our *attitude*. Let us remove animosity from our hearts. Let us remove bitterness. Let us learn to forgive. Let us pray, "God, make us compassionate people!"

THE TEST OF TOTAL CARE: "AS YOURSELF"

Before I close, I will say a word or two about the third part of the command: "As yourself." An understanding of this phrase can underline many of the truths we have tried to emphasize.

How do we love ourselves? There are a few exceptions, but most of us do *not* look at ourselves in the mirror and say, "I love you, I love you, I love you (kiss, kiss, kiss)." Rather we take care of our needs. After Paul said men are "to love their own wives as their own bodies," he explained what he meant: "No one ever hated his own flesh, but *nourishes and cherishes it*" (Ephesians 5:28, 29; emphasis mine). To love others as we love ourselves is to be unselfish enough to supply their needs.

On the other hand, this love for self usually includes some basic feeling of concern for self. Normally emotion is involved. Even so, a feeling of caring needs to be cultivated in our relationships with others, even our enemies.

As I think of loving self, I think of a passage that summarizes what it means to love one's neighbor, although the phrase "love your neighbor" is not found in it. The passage is a familiar one: "Therefore, however you want people to treat you, so treat them, for this is the Law and the Prophets" (Matthew 7:12). This is the familiar Golden Rule, usually phrased: "Do unto others as you would have them do unto you."

How do I know that this summarizes "the second great commandment"? I know it by laying several passages side by side. In Matthew 22:40, after Jesus gave the two laws on love, He said, "On these two commandments depend the whole Law and the Prophets." In Romans 13:9, 10, Paul said that if one loves his neighbor, he fulfills the law. Again he said in Galatians 5:14 the law was fulfilled in the command to love one's neighbor. Compare these passages with Matthew 7:12, where Jesus says "the Law and the Prophets" are summed up in the Golden Rule. If the command to love your neighbor summarizes the law, and the Golden Rule summarizes the law, then the command to love your neighbor must mean basically the same as the command to "do unto others" as we would have them do unto us. As the old algebraic equation says: "Things equal to the same thing are equal to each other."

THE TEST OF THE GOLDEN RULE: "AS YOURSELF" INCLUDES PATIENCE AND UNDERSTANDING

But what does it mean to treat others as we would like to be treated? Let me stress one thing at this time: I like to be treated with *patience and understanding*. Therefore, I need to treat others with patience and understanding.

Isn't that how you like others to treat you? You are not perfect. I am not perfect. But we are trying. So we would like for people to be patient with us. We would like for people to try to understand why we are the way we are and why we do the things we do.

So that means we should treat others that way, even our enemies. We need to be so patient. We need to be so understanding. That does not mean we will condone in others what is wrong; it does mean we will better be able to relate to them and help them. It does mean we will try to understand what makes them tick. "With all humility and gentleness, with patience, showing forbearance to one another in love" (Ephesians 4:2). "Love covers a multitude of sins" (1 Peter 4:8).

To make this chapter as practical as possible, I would like for you to think of one person whom you find it hard to love. I would like for you to think of that person as the special test of your love, whether your love is real or not. Determine to concentrate the next few weeks (or months or years) on learning to love that person—and to show your love. This exercise will expand your soul in a way nothing else can.

Class Discussion and Activity

1. Go through the chapter and see if you can find the eight times the command to "love your neighbor" is found in the New Testament. (If you desire, you can look up "love" and "neighbor" in a concordance.) Read and study each reference in context.
2. Discuss the parable of the Good Samaritan (Luke 10:30-37) and the many lessons it teaches. Give special attention to the *tests* the Samaritan's love was put to.
3. Discuss the challenge Jesus gave concerning loving our enemies (Matthew 5:43-48). Since in this life none of us can be "perfect" in the sense of being sinless, what does it mean to "be perfect, as your heavenly Father is perfect"?
4. Is it *natural* to love our enemies? How then can

we obey Jesus' command?

5. On a piece of paper, list the *negative* aspects of loving our enemies (what we will *not* do if we love them) and the *positive* aspects (what we *will* do). (You may want to do this together in class on the chalkboard.)

6. Study Romans 12:19-21. What does it mean to "heap burning coals" on an enemy's head?

7. Is it hard to have *a good attitude* as we help an enemy? How can we develop a better attitude toward our enemies?

8. Discuss "the golden rule" (Matthew 7:12) and all its implications in how we treat people.

9. The author put special stress on being patient and understanding. Do *we* like people to be patient with us—and to try to understand us?

10. The chapter closes with a challenge to think of one specific individual we find hard to love—and to work on *learning* to love that person. You may want to make this a class project, with each discussing what helps and what does not. (Do not have each name the person who is his or her special project.)

9
Two to Get Ready

Not everyone will or should get married. Jesus was not married. Neither was Paul. And Paul even encouraged some not to get married because of special circumstances (1 Corinthians 7).

Most, however, will get married. Most of us need to get married. In Matthew 19:10-12, it is implied that most of us are not so constituted as to remain both unmarried and pure. In 1 Corinthians 7:2, Paul said, "Because of immoralities, let each man have his own wife, and let each woman have her own husband." The KJV has, "To avoid fornication, let every man have his own wife, . . ." The fact is that most of us are either married or plan to get married. Neale Pryor, professor of Bible at Harding University, has a favorite story on this point:

> A couple came to church right before Sunday School and wanted the preacher to preach the wedding for them. He said, "We are about to have Sunday School and church, but if you will sit

through the Sunday School and church, I will be glad to oblige you when church service is over." So they patiently sat through Sunday School and church. Right at the end of the service, before the closing prayer, the preacher said, "After prayer, those wishing to get married please come forward, and I will be glad to visit with you." At the conclusion of the prayer, one man and thirty-seven women came forward.[1]

The story always gets a laugh when Neale tells it— especially from the men—but most men *and* women plan to get married someday.

What I want to talk about in this chapter is *preparing* for marriage. Sadly, most do not. One of our favorite fairy tales through the years has gone like this:

> Step 1—Nothing much ever happened to her. She had been living a life with innocent waiting, doing her schoolwork, being nice to her mother, helping with the dishes, and washing her hair every Saturday night. She was sweet and winsom and went entirely undiscovered until . . .
> Step 2—Suddenly, he appeared. He knew at once she was for him. He saw her across the room and said to himself, "I'm going to marry that girl." He was all that she had ever dreamed of: tall, dark, handsome and with a shy grin that lit up his face, and so . . .
> Step 3—They fell in love. Completely, utterly, suddenly in love. One minute she was alone in the world, an unclaimed treasure; next she was madly in love. Before he entered the room, he was adrift; no one to tie to, no good woman to keep him from going to the dogs. The next moment, there she was. And so naturally . . .

---

[1]Neale Pryor, "So You Want to Get Married," *The Preacher's Periodical*, April 1983, 7.

Step 4—They met, kissed, and knew they were meant for each other. Then, of course, there was no alternative but . . .

Step 5—They marry as soon as they can, for this is the real thing. Love is all that matters. Out of all the world, there is one man for one woman and when they are brought together by the hand of fate, they must obey and marry before it is too late. The ending of the story is always the same . . .

Step 6—They live happily ever after. If they run into trouble, then it couldn't have been real love after all, for real love means only permanent bliss. A life with never a cross word, never a dull moment, only that never-ending thrill of belonging to each other.[2]

Even in the immoral climate of today, most believe if they can just find "the right one," they will live happily ever after. In other words, it is not that important to prepare for marriage or to work at marriage after the ceremony. The important thing is to find the right one—a real soul mate. As an illustration, note those who keep marrying and divorcing and marrying and divorcing—in the vain search for just the right one.

Today many spend more care in choosing a new car than they do in choosing a mate for life. Many spend more time in preparing to pass their driving test than they do in preparing for marriage.

Several years ago, I decided that I did not wish to be just a person who performed wedding ceremonies; I wanted to help couples start marriage in the right way. Consequently, I normally require a minimum of

---

[2]Duvall in *Life and Love* quoted in Prentice A. Meador, Jr., "The Gospel According to Love," in *Voices of Action*, ed. James L. Lovell (Austin, Tex.: R. B. Sweet, 1968), 148-49.

3½ hours in premarital counseling if both the man and the woman are faithful Christians, and a minimum of 6½ hours if one or both are not. But many who contact me to perform their ceremony are unwilling to spend that much time. They will spend hours looking for a place to live and taking care of other details. Multiple hours and dollars will be spent on planning an elaborate wedding. But many are unwilling to spend a few hours on preparing to live together as husband and wife!

In his book *Marriage, Divorce, and Purity*, Joe Schubert notes that to get ready for marriage properly, there needs to be physical preparation, intellectual preparation, vocational preparation, emotional preparation, moral preparation, and spiritual preparation. I wish I had time to speak of all these; each one is important and makes a positive contribution to a happy and God-pleasing marriage. But at this time, I want to discuss *the most important aspect* of preparing for marriage.

What would *you* consider the most important part of preparation for marriage? The most important preparation is suggested by one of our basic texts, one to which we have returned again and again: "And He said to him, 'You shall love the Lord your God with all your heart, and with all your soul, and with all your mind.' This is the great and foremost commandment. The second is like it, 'You shall love your neighbor as yourself.'" The thought I want to pull from these verses is expressed in the title of Thomas Warren's book: *Marriage Is for Those Who* [1] *Love God* [2] *—and One Another*. I want to stress two key words: "priorities" and "commitment." Let me suggest that if you want a happy, God-pleasing marriage, two things are necessary: (1) commitment to God and (2) commitment to each other. The more important of these two is commitment to God.

COMMITMENT TO GOD

That comment will surprise some, but that is what Jesus says in Matthew 22:37, 38. The most important thing in life—and that includes marriage—is loving *God* with all your being. The same point is made by Jesus in Luke 14:26: "If anyone comes to Me, and does not hate [love less] his own father and mother and wife and children and brothers and sisters, yes, and even his own life, he cannot be My disciple." Charles Hodge says that the most important criteria in choosing a mate is this: *Marry someone who loves God more than he or she loves you.*[3] He says that you can trust this person. You know that this person will do what is right, whatever the circumstances.

The longer I try to help couples get ready for marriage, the more I am convinced that unless both of them love God and are committed to Him, the commitment they make to each other amounts to little. I never marry anyone without first asking them if they believe marriage is for life. To this point, I have never had anyone say, "No, I do not believe that marriage is for life." Why then do many of the marriages of those who have thus answered end in divorce? I am convinced that nothing backs up their commitment to the marriage. It is as if I had asked them if they believed

---

[3]Charles B. Hodge, Jr., "The Beatitudes and Marriage," *The Preacher's Periodical*, June 1983, 11.

Richard Nixon would be a great President. They reply, "Sure!" Later, however, they acknowledge, "Okay, so we were wrong." Even so, they say, "Yes, we really believe that marriage is for life!" But later: "Well, we were wrong on that point."

Unless a person believes that when he is married, he is married in the sight of God as well as in the sight of man,[4] unless he is unwilling to break the heart of God by disobedience, unless all his decisions are based on the desire to obey God in every way so he can spend eternity with Him, the marriage certificate is not worth the paper it is printed on, and the vows are not worth the time it takes to say them.

On the other hand, if both the bride and the groom are sincerely committed to the Lord, there is no better start to marriage. One study indicated that 97 per cent of broken marriages involve one or both partners who do not attend church services regularly. On the contrary, only 1 in 57 marriages of those who attend worship regularly break up. Furthermore, only 1 in 500 marriages of people deeply committed to God break up in divorce![5]

It is possible that the phrase "committed to God" may be too vague for you to really understand what I am saying. Let me make it as simple as I can:

First, BE a Christian, a dedicated Christian.

Charles Hodge calls this the other side of the coin. If you need to marry someone who loves God more than you, the person you marry also needs someone who loves God more than him or her.

When I say "be a Christian" I do not mean just be

---

[4]Matthew 19:6.
[5]Statistics are from a recent *Pulpit Helps* (6815 Shallowford Road, Chattanooga, TN 37422).

someone who has been baptized.[6] I do not mean just be someone who attends some of the worship services of the church[7]—maybe because someone has made you or you wanted to impress someone. Rather I mean a growing, serious, Bible-reading, praying, sharing Christian, one who is living the life of one following Jesus! To make this as practical as possible, let me note that this includes learning to exercise self-control regarding the sexual drive.

> For this is the will of God, your sanctification; that is, that you abstain from sexual immorality; that each of you know how to possess his own vessel in sanctification and honor, not in lustful passion, like the Gentiles who do not know God (1 Thessalonians 4:3-5).

Be a virgin when you marry—whether you are a man or a woman. You will please God. It will make your marriage better. It will help your marriage to last.

But not only be a Christian,

Second, MARRY a Christian, a dedicated Christian—not just someone on a church roll somewhere. Marry someone who has the same convictions you do about marriage. Marry someone who will work as hard at the marriage as you will. Marry someone who will be the best possible mother or father for your children.

In the Old Testament, God's people were commanded not to marry those outside the faith (Deuteronomy 7:3, 4), and dire things happened when that commandment was disobeyed (1 Kings 11:1, 2). In the

---

[6]Although that is essential to being a Christian according to Mark 16:16; Acts 2:38; Galatians 3:26, 27.

[7]This, too, is important (Hebrews 10:25).

New Testament, we find the same emphasis. Paul said a widow is to marry "only in the Lord" (1 Corinthians 7:39). Paul said he had a right to marry a sister, a fellow Christian (1 Corinthians 9:5). And Paul said not to be unequally yoked with unbelievers:

> Do not be bound together with unbelievers; for what partnership have righteousness and lawlessness, or what fellowship has light with darkness? Or what harmony has Christ with Belial, or what has a believer in common with an unbeliever? (2 Corinthians 6:14, 15).

This passage may include more than the marriage vow, but surely it includes marriage. There is no "binding" more constraining, with more pressures to conform, than marriage.

Neale Pryor notes that each of us ought to marry a Christian for the sake of the Scriptures, for the sake of our souls, for the sake of our homes, for the sake of our children.[8] I am sick at heart with lovely Christian young men and young women marrying non-Christians with no spiritual values because "he says he has changed" or "I think I can help him." If you *love God*, you will marry someone who will help you be the kind of Christian you ought to be!

Based on this commitment, we come to priority number two and commitment number two.

COMMITMENT TO EACH OTHER

The second commandment is to love (*agapao*) your neighbor as yourself (Matthew 22:39). This refers to

---

[8]Pryor, 7-12.

138

everyone. Certainly, right at the top of the list of people we should love should be the ones we marry.

The importance of this was stressed by Paul. In just a handful of verses in Ephesians 5, Paul used the word "love" (*agapao*) four times in referring to the way a husband is to relate to his wife.

> Husbands, love your wives, just as Christ also loved the church and gave Himself up for her; . . . So husbands ought also to love their own wives as their own bodies. He who loves his own wife loves himself; for no one ever hated his own flesh, but nourishes and cherishes it, just as Christ also does the church, . . . Let each individual among you also love his own wife even as himself; and let the wife see to it that she respect her husband (vv. 25, 28, 29, 33).

Notice also Colossians 3:18, 19: "Wives, be subject to your husbands, as is fitting in the Lord. Husbands, love your wives, and do not be embittered against them." Or to turn the matter around, in Titus 2:4 young women are to be taught "to love their husbands, to love their children."

Most of these references use some form of the word *agape* for "love." We have been stressing that love "seeks the best" for the one loved. In this chapter, let us also stress that *agape* love is *commitment* love. It is unselfish. It is unconditional. It requires no response. It is a deliberate act of the will. It is a *commitment* to do what is right, to be what is right, to seek the best for the one to whom the commitment is made.

This type of commitment is spoken of in both the Old and New Testaments. For instance, in the Old Testament, we have these words in the Song of Solomon:

Put me like a seal over your heart,
Like a seal on your arm.
For love is as strong as death, . . .
Its flashes are flashes of fire,
The very flame of the Lord.
Many waters cannot quench love,
Nor will rivers overflow it;
If a man were to give all the riches
    of his house for love,
It would be utterly despised (8:6, 7).

Jesus spoke of this commitment in the New Testament in Matthew 19:

Have you not read, that He who created them from the beginning made them male and female, and said, "For this cause a man shall leave his father and mother, and shall cleave to his wife; and the two shall become one flesh"? Consequently they are no longer two, but one flesh (vv. 4-6a).

The word "cleave" in this passage literally means "to be glued to." Today, instead of "cleave," we would probably use the words "be committed to." Jesus stressed that this commitment is *for life*: "What therefore God has joined together, let no man separate. . . . I say to you, whoever divorces his wife, except for immorality, and marries another woman commits adultery" (vv. 6b, 9). Note that this commitment to one's mate (commitment number two) is based on commitment to God (commitment number one), a realization that *God* joins the two together—for life.

Is it a commitment for as long as our marriage "works out"? No, it is for life!

Is it a commitment that is conditional on his becoming what I want him to be? No, it is for life!

140

Is it a commitment that is binding as long as he (or she) *stays* as I like? No, it is for life!

It is this commitment that makes a marriage work. The marriage license is important. We are to abide by the laws of the land (Romans 13:1ff.; 1 Peter 2:13-15). But a marriage license alone will not make a marriage work. Marriage ceremonies, vows, and rings have value. They can help impress on our minds what marriage is all about. But ceremonies, vows, and rings will not make a marriage work. What makes a marriage work is this commitment for life. The marriage works because it *has* to work.

Which brings me to a discussion of how the different types of love contribute to a marriage. It will sound as if I have left the subject of commitment for a while, but stay with me. I assure you I have not.

Let me briefly review three of the four Greek words for "love." Think back to what we said about these words. I will use the noun forms. *Eros* we designated as "physical attraction." This is "Strawberry Shortcake Love." *Philia* is "friendship love." We called this "Bowling Team Love." *Agape* is "seeks-the-best love" or "Rain-on-the-Just-and-the-Unjust Love." In this chapter we are stressing it is *commitment* love.

Let us see how these three types of love fit into the biblical concept of marriage. Let us begin by talking about *courtship* habits.

Courtship customs vary, but in Western civilization, *we generally start with eros*. Something attracts us about the other person. A nice smile. An attractive appearance. A pleasant personality. Something.

Within itself, this is not bad. God made men where they are attracted to women and women where they are attracted to men. That is part of God's plan to

141

assure the continuation of the human race. It is a starting place. But God intended that we should build on that something more substantial.

Unfortunately, this is as far as some couples go. Their entire relationship consists of episodes in dark places, parked cars, perhaps even bedrooms. Sometimes the argument is made, "If you really love me, you'll go to bed with me." The one who makes that argument knows only of *eros* love.

More unfortunately, some get married on the basis of *eros* love. After the honeymoon, they wake up to find they are married to a stranger. The typical marriage relationship is 70 per cent talk and there is little chance that these can sustain this. Their marriage is off to the worst possible start.

Remember that *eros* love is "Strawberry Shortcake Love." It is a love primarily interested in consumption. But after the consumption is completed, one loses interest. During the summer, I enjoyed a watermelon with other members of my family. It was really a great watermelon. Cold, sweet, juicy. The juice ran down my arms and dripped on my shoes. But guess what? After my third or fourth big slice, I lost interest in that watermelon.

We have a classic example of this kind of "love" in 2 Samuel 13 where Amnon was filled with desire for his half-sister Tamar. Verses 1 and 2 say that he loved her so much that it made him sick. But it was just *eros* love. In verse 14, he forces her to "make love" to him. Now listen to verse 15: "Then Amnon hated her with a very great hatred; for the hatred with which he hated her was greater than the love with which he had loved her. And Amnon said to her, 'Get up, go away!'" He had made himself sick on shortcake; now he wanted it out of his sight. That is the way it is when all you have going for you is *eros*. Marriages based solely on *eros* will generally last six months to two years.

But, if things work as they should, *after the initial mutual attraction, the couple develops* **philia** *love*. They get acquainted with each other and find that they *like* each other. They enjoy being with each other. They enjoy doing things together. They enjoy talking together. They have fun together.

Again, within itself, this is good. It is not good for a man to be alone (Genesis 2:18); we all need friends. The one we marry should be our best friend. When Titus 2:4 speaks of loving one's husband, the word used is a form of *philia*. But unfortunately, some get married without their love ever progressing beyond the *philia* stage. Again, their marriage is in trouble.

First, *philia* love makes no provision for the unattractive part of our personalities. All of us have character quirks or irritating habits. Before marriage, these may be something to laugh about or even to call "cute." But in the close ties of marriage, these can take on gigantic proportions.

Second, *philia* love makes little or no provision for changes in personality. All of us are in a constant state of change. I am not the same nineteen-year-old boy Jo married. In some ways I may be better. In some ways I am definitely worse. But one thing is certain: I have changed. And "friendship love" alone makes little provision for such change.

Remember that *philia* love is "Bowling Team Love." This fellow is on our bowling team. He has a great personality; he is a great bowler. We are glad to have him on the team. But for some reason or another, he becomes abusive, and it begins to affect his game. He is no longer any fun to be around, and his bowling score is pulling down the whole team. What do we do? "For the good of the team," we dump him.

Even so, many couples say, "We're no longer compatible. . . . Marriage is not any fun anymore. . . . We no longer have anything in common. . . . We've grown apart." Therefore, "for the good of everyone concerned," they dump each other. (If you have ever been dumped, you know what I mean.)

Marriages based solely on *eros* and *philia* love, that progress no further, will generally last seven to fifteen years—because most marriages have crisis periods at somewhere around seven to fifteen years.

But if everything goes as God intends it should *in the courtship, the couple will finally proceed to* **agape** *love*. Each will decide on one person. Each will get to know that one person well. Each will decide, "I want to spend the rest of my life with that one person." Then each will *commit* himself to spend the rest of his life with that one person . . . to always care for, protect, and love that one person, to always seek the best for that one person . . . *no matter what*.

Remember that *agape* love is "Rain-on-the-Just-and-the-Unjust Love." It does not bestow love because the other person is always lovable, but because a commitment was made to always love the other person!

Marriages based on *eros, philia,* and *agape* love on the part of both marriage partners will last a lifetime.

This then is the usual order and progression of courtship in Western civilization, if one makes it to *agape* love. We start with *eros* attraction. We develop *philia* friendship. Finally, we make an *agape* commitment. You might think of it as a pyramid with *eros* at the base and *agape* at the apex.

Now let us come to *marriage*. In lasting marriages, the order reverses. The base becomes *agape*, and resting on it are *philia* and *eros*.

Each layer of our pyramid is important. *Eros* is important. In marriage, two are to become one flesh (Genesis 2:24; Matthew 19:5). A mutually satisfying physical relationship is an important part of God's plan for marriage (1 Corinthians 7:2-5). If a young couple planning to get married do not already have good literature on the subject written from a Christian viewpoint, I give them some.

But this *eros* love needs to be tied in with *philia* love and *agape* love so that it is an expression of love and concern for the other person. When that is the case, *eros* love enhances and beautifies the marriage.

Philia love is also important. We have already suggested that our mates should be our best friends. In this regard, I like Proverbs 17:17: "A friend loves at all times." A biblical example of a husband and wife having friendship love is Aquila and Priscilla (Acts 18:2, 26ff.). They sewed tents together. They had home Bible studies together. They worked together with Paul. They got kicked out of Rome together. This is an aspect of married love all of us have to continue to work on, to continue to enjoy doing things together. One special need is to learn to really *communicate* with our mates.

Again, *philia* love should not stand alone. It needs to be tied in with *agape* love. If it is, then *philia* love can make a marriage so special.

The most important love in marriage, however, is *agape* love, commitment love. This love is not "I love you because . . ." or "I'll love if . . ." It is simply "I love you." This kind of love does not have to be reciprocated. This kind of love does what it should whether the other person does or not.

Many keep their eyes closed to the shortcomings of their intended before they get married, and their eyes are forced open after they are married. *Agape* love has its eyes wide open before the marriage, as it strives to make a God-pleasing decision. Then, in a sense, it closes its eyes after marriage. The biblical way of expressing this is found in 1 Peter 4:8: "Love covers a multitude of sins."

When a marriage is based on *agape* love, there is always hope for that marriage. Sometimes people come to me, all torn up, saying, "I don't love my husband (or wife) any more!" Generally what they mean by that is the *eros* and *philia* part of their marriage is messed up. They are no longer attracted to their mates. They may not even like their mates at that point in time. I try to ascertain whether the *agape* foundation is still intact. Is there still concern for the well-being of the other person? Do they still have any sense of commitment? If they do, the other aspects of love can be rebuilt, especially if both parties desire it. They can return to their old courtship habits and rebuild a special feeling for each other. It takes time. A couple does not get their marriage in a mess over a period of eight years and then undo that in five easy sessions. But the marriage *can* be rebuilt.

*The key is the foundation of **agape** love, this commitment to each other!*

CONCLUSION

In closing, let me return to the two matters of priorities and commitment. Imagine that you and your mate or mate-to-be are standing before me, ready to be married. A number of things will be done in the ceremony, but two things will be of prime importance. Near the first, I will mention that we are "present in the sight of God." There needs to be a sense of being in God's presence and a desire to please Him. There needs to be a commitment *to God*. Then, when time has come for the vows, I will ask each of you, "Do you promise to love, honor, and cherish him (or her) in sickness and in health, in prosperity and in distress, as long as you both shall live?" This is commitment *to each other*.

We are not just talking about words. We are not talking about following some traditional form. We are talking about commitment for life. If you want a happy, God-pleasing marriage and if you want you and your mate and your children to go to heaven someday, you had better mean it!

Please pray with me:

> Almighty God, the One Who made us and who instituted marriage to bless our lives, forgive us for failing to make marriage what it should be, all it can be. Be with those of us who are already married. Forgive us for taking our mates for granted. Help us to renew our commitment to one another. Help us to learn to show love to one another in every way. Be with those who are thinking about getting married. Help them find someone who will bless their lives and draw them closer to You. Help them prepare for their marriage. Help them to be really committed to You— and to each other. In Jesus' name, Amen.

Class Discussion and Activity

1. Joe Schubert suggests that before marriage, six kinds of preparation need to be made: physical, intellectual, vocational, emotional, moral, and spiritual. Discuss what each of these areas would include. (Optional: Have someone read the pertinent section in his book *Marriage, Divorce, and Purity* and report on what he says about these areas.)

2. Why do you think such a rapid increase in divorce has taken place in recent years? Do you think that real commitment—to God and to each other—is lacking in many (most?) marriages today?

3. Why do you think such a rapid increase in sexual immorality has taken place in recent years, both before marriage and after people are married? What reasons would you give a young person for remaining sexually pure before marriage?

4. How important is it to teach our children to marry Christians? Discuss the Old and New Testament passages that deal with this subject.

5. Many believe they can be married "in the sight of God" without obeying civil laws regarding marriage. Does the Bible teach that we are to obey the laws of the land?

6. According to the author, how long will a marriage based solely on *eros* love last? One based only on *eros* and *philia* love? One based on *agape* love? Can you think of any illustrations of these statistics?

7. Review the meaning of the Greek words *eros*, *philia*, and *agape* from chapter 2 ("The Greeks Have a Word for It"), and be prepared to discuss

the place each has in courtship and then in marriage.

8. Optional: If appropriate, share the titles of helpful books on sex written from a "Christian" standpoint. The author gives a paperback book *The Act of Marriage* to his counselees and recommends *Intended for Pleasure*.

9. If you have several in your class who have been married many years, ask them to share the "secret" of staying married. (Listen for words that relate to the concept of commitment.)

10. The author suggests that as long as the commitment (*agape*) base remains, physical attraction (*eros*) and friendship (*philia*) can be restored to a marriage—if both are willing to work at it. Discuss how a couple can relearn to enjoy each other.

11. Suggested class project: Buy a copy of this book for each couple getting married. Put a note in the front for them to give special attention to chapters 2, 9, and 10.

10
The Heart of the Home

If love exists anywhere, it should exist in our homes. Next to salvation and a relationship with God, there is no greater need in the world today than the need for homes in which love dwells. It is a dog-eat-dog world. If we have a haven to which we can come at the end of the day, a haven where there is concern and sympathy and love, we can make it. But if we go home to more hassle than happiness, it gets rough to go on day after day.

In the Bible the word "house" appears ten times as often as the word "home." Is there any significance in that? Were there ten times as many houses as homes? I do not know, but I *do* know that some homes today are just boarding houses with carpet and TV. And I know that we need homes desperately today—homes in which biblical love abounds.

WE NEED TO LOVE EACH OTHER
IN THE HOME

The wise man said, "Better is a dish of vegetables where love is, than a fattened ox and hatred with it" (Proverbs 15:17). The KJV reads "a stalled ox." This is top-quality beef from steers fattened in the feedlot, not that tough, stringy stuff from animals that have been butchered right off the range. It is thick, rich, red meat with little streaks of white fat running through it. It gives those who worry about cholesterol nightmares, but melts in your mouth as it comes hot off the grill. Solomon says, however, if you have to be in the company of people who cannot stand you to get it, you are better off with a bowl of beans and cornbread if you eat those beans with people who love you.

Money and possessions and the best cuts of meat do not make a home. It is a place to be together and love, no matter what happens to be in the cupboard. In Hosea 11:4, God speaks of the "bonds of love." A real home has many bonds of love.

In the last chapter, we talked of the need for a bride and groom to love each other and to make a life-time commitment to each other. The Bible teaches, however, that not only should the husband and wife love each other, but *each one in the home should love the others*. Let us go to God's original family-life Manual to show that this is so. We will begin with Mom and Dad because this is the main way the children learn what love is all about.

Dad is to love Mom. The most important thing any man can do for his children is to love their mother. Note these passages in the Old Testament:

Then Isaac . . . took Rebekah, and she became his wife; and he loved her; . . . (Genesis 24:67).

Now Jacob loved Rachel, so he said [to his father-in-law, Laban], "I will serve you seven years for your younger daughter Rachel." . . . So Jacob served seven years for Rachel and they seemed to him but a few days because of his love for her (Genesis 29:18, 20).

[Speaking of Elkanah:] To Hannah he would give a double portion, for he loved Hannah, . . . (1 Samuel 1:5).

And the king loved Esther. . . . (Esther 2:17).

. . . rejoice in the wife of your youth. . . . Be exhilarated always with her love (Proverbs 5:18, 19).

Enjoy life with the woman [wife, KJV] whom you love all the days of your fleeting life which He has given to you under the sun; . . . (Ecclesiastes 9:9).

[The bride says of the groom:] . . . his banner over me is love (Song of Solomon 2:4).

The greatest challenge of all is found in the New Testament in Ephesians 5 (and repeated in Colossians 3:19):

Husbands, love your wives, just as Christ also loved the church and gave Himself up for her; . . . So husbands ought also to love their own wives as their own bodies. . . . Let each individual among you also love his own wife even as himself; . . . (vv. 25, 28, 33).

Men are to love their wives as Christ loved the church! Think of all Christ did for the church. His thoughts were not for Himself, but for the church. He gave up heaven and came to earth to establish the church. In His love, He was totally unselfish, totally giving, and totally serving. Finally, He died for the church. As I think about this, I can only ask all to pray for those of us who are husbands as we face this almost impossible challenge!

Mom is also to love Dad. Here are two pertinent passages:

> Michal, Saul's daughter, loved David. . . . (1 Samuel 18:20).

> Older women . . . are to . . . encourage the young women to love their husbands, to love their children (Titus 2:3, 4).

Both Mom and Dad are to love the kids. Young women are to be encouraged "to love their children."

In Psalms 127:3, we are told that children are a blessing: "Children are a gift of the Lord; the fruit of the womb is a reward." Thus we often read in the Scriptures of parents loving their children (not always acting wisely on their love, but loving them). Abraham loved Isaac (Genesis 22:2). Isaac loved Esau, Rebekah loved Jacob (Genesis 25:28), and Jacob loved Joseph (Genesis 37:3). Exodus 21:5 speaks of a slave, having been released, choosing to remain a slave because of his love for his wife and his children.

I think we could even use Matthew 10:37 here, though it is negative in its thrust. Jesus says, "He who loves father or mother more than Me is not worthy of Me; and he who loves son or daughter more than Me is not worthy of Me." Jesus says that our first priority must be love for Him, but note the assumption. The assumption is that we will love our sons and daughters.

To turn it around, *the kids are to love Mom and Dad.* Note Matthew 10:37 again. It assumes that we will love father and mother.

When Paul listed the terrible sins of his day, he included being "unloving" (Romans 1:31; 2 Timothy 3:3). This word is translated from the negative form of the word *storge*—family love. The KJV translates the word as "without natural affection." This would include the natural affection one should have for those of his own family. Jesus gave an example of this in Matthew 15 when He spoke of some using a man-made tradition to absolve themselves from taking care of their mothers and fathers.

Let me also say that *kid number one in the family should love kid number two and kid number three and so on.* Luke 14:26 is Luke's account of the statement Jesus made in Matthew 10:37—and it includes brothers and sisters.

The bottom line is that everybody in the family should love everybody else in the family. How we need homes like that!

WHAT IT MEANS TO LOVE EACH OTHER IN THE HOME

To make our lesson as practical as possible, let me ask: What does it *mean* to love each other in the home?

At the risk of sounding like a broken record, I will say again that in the original Greek text, most of the references on love in the New Testament use the word *agape*—and that *agape* love *seeks the best for* the one loved.

The implications of this are far-reaching regarding the home, but time will allow me to only stress one point: *Love supplies needs.* In his excellent book on friendship evangelism called *Concentric Circles of Concern,* W. Oscar Thompson, Jr., makes this point again and again. As he summarizes the point, he says:

> Love is
> NOT a word of emotion,
> NOT a word of feeling.
>
> Rather, love is
> A word of reason,
> A word of volition or will,
> A word of action,
> Love is doing!
>
> Love *builds* relationships;
> Love *maintains* relationships;
> Love *fulfills* relationships;
> Love *initiates* relationships;
>
> Love is *meeting needs!*[1]

Love supplies *needs,* God-approved needs, not necessarily all *wants.* Love's primary purpose is not to change others, but to meet their needs. When a change is needed, love works indirectly, showing concern and reinforcing what is good. *Agape* love is unselfish, not concerned with self but concerned with the other person. "Through love serve one another" (Galatians 5:13).

When I say that love supplies needs, I mean any need. For instance, love is concerned with *physical needs.*

The husband is to love his wife as his own body (Ephesians 5:28). Our bodies have physical needs, and we try to supply those needs. Even so, one who loves

---

[1] W. Oscar Thompson, Jr., *Concentric Circles of Concern* (Nashville: Broadman Press, 1981), 101.

will "provide for his own" (1 Timothy 5:8).

The father who works hard to make a living is expressing love. The mother who keeps the house clean and prepares good meals—often in addition to another job—is expressing love.

Perhaps this would be a good place to ask: Do we *appreciate* these expressions of love? Often we take such for granted, not really considering these as expressions of love, when others, who do not have someone to take care of them, would give most anything to be loved in that fashion!

Love is also concerned about *emotional needs*.

All of us have emotional needs. We need to know that we are loved. We need to know that we are accepted. We need to know that we are secure. And we need reassurance of these things from time to time.

So learn to *express* your love. Express it in words. Husbands and wives, the Song of Solomon is your manual on expressing love to each other. Read it together. If you feel like it, laugh together over some of the ways of expressing love in the past—but do not miss the point. They *said* they loved each other. The phrase "my love" (in other words, my loved one) is found over a dozen times in the book. They also complimented each other. Husbands, take note of how chapter 4 begins: "How beautiful you are, my darling, how beautiful you are!"

Also express your love in actions. Remember 1 John 3:18: "Let us not love with word or with tongue [only], but in deed and truth." Wives and husbands, there is kissing in our Manual: "May he kiss me with the kisses of his mouth! . . . His mouth is full of sweetness. . . ." (Song of Solomon 1:2; 5:16). And there is hugging. "Let . . . his right hand embrace me" (Song of Solomon

8:3). One doctor suggests we all need at least four hugs a day—and he even writes prescriptions for it. But he always notes that it is OK to go over the prescribed number. "No one ever died from a hug overdose," he says.

How mothers and fathers need to learn to express their love to each other! Most marriages do not die from a blowout, but from a slow leak—as we neglect the little things that say, "I love you."

This should not be limited to Mom and Dad expressing love to each other. The children also need to know that the parents love them, and the parents need to know that the children love them.

As we are talking about love supplying needs, let us not forget *spiritual needs*. If love really "seeks the best," it cannot neglect the spiritual, for this is the most important need of all.

If I love members of my family, as the head of my home (Ephesians 5:23; 6:1), I will see that they are taught God's Word. I will make sure they are always in Bible class and worship service. I will teach them myself. Jesus said, "It is written in the prophets, 'And they shall all be taught of God.' Everyone who has heard and learned from the Father, comes to Me" (John 6:45).

As we are thinking about needs, let us stress that everyone in the family has special needs. Dad has his own special needs.[2] He needs a wife whose one desire in life is to please him and to make him a successful husband and father. He needs a wife who reverences him as God's authority in the home (Ephesians 5:22, 23). He needs a wife who will train their children to be

---

[2]This list is adapted from Gary Beauchamp.

loyal and loving to God and to their father. He needs the physical love of his wife. Some time ago, I clipped this little story from the *Reader's Digest*, written by an over-busy wife:

> After I had taken on a few too many projects, my responsibilities began piling upon me. To keep my forgetfulness to a minimum, I started a daily reminder list, scratching off items as I completed them. Some two weeks later I bragged to my husband, Clarence, "Thanks to that list I have never once overlooked a single important detail."
>
> Not long afterward I returned home from a late-night meeting and picked up my list to check on the next day's activities. There, in my husband's handwriting, wedged between "1:30— hair appointment," and "Clean the linen closet," was the notation: "Seduce Clarence."

Mom has some special needs.[3] She needs a husband who accepts his responsibilities as spiritual leader of the home. She needs a husband who loves her with a sacrificial devotion (remember that husbands are to love their wives as Christ loves the church). She needs to know that her husband is a one-woman man.

Is it not sad that we have to stress that last point today? The Bible still says, "You shall not commit adultery" (Romans 13:9). The difference between "loyalty" and "disloyalty" is not D-I-S but L-O-V-E.

Mom also needs genuine praise; she needs to feel appreciated. As the description of the worthy woman draws near the close in Proverbs 31, it is noted that "her husband . . . praises her" (v. 28). First Peter 3:7 tells husbands to "grant . . . honor" to their wives.

---

[3]Also adapted from Gary Beauchamp. The list for children is my own.

Incidentally, part of a wife's feeling appreciated is to know that her opinions are valued.

The *kids* have special needs. They need two parents who love each other. They need parents who love them—and who let them know they are loved. Not because they are beautiful . . . or talented . . . or popular . . . or even good . . . but just because they are part of the family. I may not always agree with everything my children do, and I have to deal with those things as best I can, but they are always my children and I love them. Can you imagine the father of the Prodigal Son sending out his wife to meet his younger son with this message: "You broke your father's heart when you left, and he never intends to talk to you again"?

They need parents who are good examples, who will *show* them what Christianity is. They need parents who care enough about them to take the time to both *teach* them and *train* them (Proverbs 22:6). Paul gave this parental challenge in Ephesians 6:4: "And, fathers, do not provoke your children to anger; but bring them up in the discipline and instruction of the Lord." Children need parents who will teach and encourage them in what is right, who will correct them when they do wrong, even punishing them if necessary.

> For those whom the Lord *loves* He disciplines, and He scourges every son whom He receives (Hebrews 12:6; emphasis mine).

> The rod and reproof give wisdom, but a child who gets his own way brings shame to his mother (Proverbs 29:15).

(Many will remember the paddle hanging on the wall with the inscription, "I need thee every hour.")

If I am really seeking the best for my child, I will want him to grow to be what he should be. That will involve some corrective discipline. If I do not do this, the Bible says I really do not love my child.

Not only does each family member have special needs, but we should also note that each one in the family has *individual* needs, those that are uniquely his or hers. This brings me to these final words about filling needs. If I am going to express my love by taking care of needs, at least three things will be necessary:

(1) I must become *sensitive* to the needs of those in my family.

Let me return to the illustration used by Paul. I am to love my wife as my own body (Ephesians 5:28). Have you ever stubbed your toe? Sure you have. I can still remember going barefoot in the summertime. At least once each summer I would stub a big toe so badly that the toenail was pulled halfway back. Hurt, pain, agony! When you stubbed your toe, were you *aware* of it? Certainly you were! What did you do? You took care of that need. Paul says our wives are to be as close to us as our own bodies. If she is hurting, we need to be sensitive enough to *know* it. Then we need to try to help the hurting.

Some businessmen work hard on being sensitive to the needs of the public so they can make a dollar. But they may have a household of people who are hurting and be totally unaware of their needs. We need to be sensitive.

(2) I must realize that *needs change.*

I cannot work out this matter of taking care of needs and think that I have done what I should, so I can forget about it and get on with something else. Love must always be filed under "unfinished business." It must be worked on from now on.

The needs of Mom and Dad change. The needs we have when we are first married differ from the needs when we have children and we are trying to survive financially. These needs differ from the needs when the children leave the home and we start getting older.

The needs of the children change. They must be taught to be more and more independent, and finally they need to be encouraged to go out on their own (Matthew 19:5). In Deuteronomy 32:11, Moses uses the illustration of a mother eagle forcing the eaglets to leave the nest and to learn to fly; he compares this with God's guidance of His people:

> Like an eagle that stirs up its nest,
> That hovers over its young,
> He spread His wings and caught them,
> He carried them on His pinions.

The time comes when children need to leave the nest. When that time comes, we need to help them do this in the least painful way. To change my metaphor, the loving parent is willing to cut the apron strings.

(3) I must realize that all this *takes time*.

It was not quite so difficult some years ago. As families, we spent more time together accidentally than most families today spend together on purpose. We ate three meals together. We talked together. Most people worked together—on the farm or in a family business. Most play-time and fun-time, what little there was, was together. But that was before the days of TV and compartmentalized lives.

It will do no good, however, to yearn for "the good old days." We must do the best we can in *these* days, under *today's* conditions. Quite simply, this means that we must *make* time to be together. We can turn off the TV and eat together. We can set aside special times for the family—maybe one night a week—and do our best to keep other things from interferring. We can let others in our family know that they are more important to us than our newspaper or Monday night football. We can let our children know that, as long as their requests are reasonable, they can interrupt us to get help or to tell us about their day.

No, we are not talking about something that is easy. We are not talking about something that will change overnight. We are talking about something worth working on and praying about. Because we are talking about *love* in the home.

CONCLUSION

Some time ago the East German government released an eight-volume Socialistic encyclopedia. In it there was a major and significant omission. There was no section on love. In contrast with that, love permeates Christianity from top to bottom, from side to side, from front to back, from stem to stern. And there is no place it is needed more than in the home. Love puts *the heart* in home.

If you have a home with few physical possessions, but one that is filled with love, you are rich indeed. But if you live in a mansion without love, you are poor.

GETTING SERIOUS ABOUT LOVE

Class Discussion and Activity

1. Do you think we need homes "where love abounds"? What are some of the results when love does not exist in a home?
2. Discuss how Jesus expressed (and continues to express) His love for the church. Apply this to how husbands should love their wives.
3. Check Romans 1:31 and 2 Timothy 3:3 in several translations. Find the word translated "unloving" in the NASV and "without natural affection" in the KJV. Give some examples of what it meant to be "without natural affection" in Paul's day (if necessary, look back at chapter 2). Is this still a problem today?
4. List the characteristics of love from 1 Corinthians 13:4-7, and then apply these to the home.
5. Do you agree that the father and the mother who provide for the needs of their family are expressing love? Do we often take such things for granted?
6. Read the Song of Solomon, and mark the many expressions of love found in the book. In class, share one or two you especially liked.
7. How important is hugging in a family? Does this come more naturally to some than to others? Can all of us *learn* to be more demonstrative?
8. Have we fully expressed love to our family if we are not concerned about the family's *spiritual* needs?
9. Men, be prepared to answer this question in class: What does a man need to feel loved? Women, be prepared to answer this question: What does a woman need to feel loved?

10. The Bible says disciplining a child who has done wrong is an expression of love. How can we help our children *know* that we love them when we discipline them?
11. Optional: In class, have each married person write on a card the words "*I feel loved when*" and then list five ways. Ask each to share this with his or her mate when they get home.

11
The Badge of Discipleship

Our minds go back over nineteen hundred years to an upper room in the city of Jerusalem. It is night—one of the darkest nights in the history of the world. It is dark—not because of clouds hiding the moon, but because it is the night of the betrayal of Jesus.[1]

It is the time for the observance of the Passover. Jesus and His disciples gather around the table in the upper room. We can feel the tenseness of the atmosphere and the sadness of the disciples as Jesus foretells His imminent death and the fact that one of His own will betray and deliver Him to His enemies. On this dramatic occasion, Jesus takes bread and fruit of the vine and institutes the Lord's Supper as a continuing memorial of His death.

But when Jesus speaks, He does not speak as a

---

[1]The first few paragraphs are adapted from George Stephenson, "Restoring the New Testament Church in Love," *1966 Fort Worth Christian College Lectures: Restoring the New Testament Church,* 106-7.

defeated man, but as one in control of Himself and His situation. To His troubled disciples, He says: "Let not your heart be troubled; believe in God, believe also in Me. In My Father's house are many dwelling places; if it were not so, I would have told you; for I go to prepare a place for you" (John 14:1, 2). Again He speaks to His anxious disciples with these words of assurance: "Peace I leave with you; My peace I give to you; not as the world gives, do I give to you. Let not your heart be troubled, nor let it be fearful" (John 14:27). Even as He faced death, He could speak of His joy: "These things I have spoken to you, that My joy may be in you, and that your joy may be made full" (John 15:11).

It is in the midst of these dramatic events that Jesus spoke these words to His disciples:

> Little children, I am with you a little while longer. You shall seek Me; and as I said to the Jews, I now say to you also, "Where I am going, you cannot come." A new commandment I give to you, that you love one another, even as I have loved you, that you also love one another. By this all men will know that you are My disciples, if you have love for one another (John 12:33-35).

Let us note first that Jesus gave His disciples a commandment.

A COMMANDMENT

Jesus said, "A new *commandment* I give to you." We are not talking about something that would merely be good or nice to do or something that is just an ideal. Rather we are talking about a commandment. This is not an optional matter. It *has* to be done.

As I surveyed all the Bible on the subject of love, I was impressed with this fact: There are more passages in the New Testament on the love that exists between brothers and sisters in Christ than there are on other aspects of love. Jesus did not want us to miss this point: We should love each other in the church.

As we look at the many passages on loving our brethren, we see that the concepts of *agape* love (an act of the will) and *philia* love (warm, emotional love) mingle. Notice for instance, 1 Peter 1:22: "Since you have in obedience to the truth purified your souls for a sincere *love of the brethren,* fervently *love one another* from the heart." (Emphasis mine.) The compound Greek word translated "love of the brethren" includes the word *philia,* while "love one another" translates a form of the word *agape.*

Generally when you see the phrase "brotherly love" or a similar phrase in the New Testament, it is a translation of *philadelphia: philia* M *adelphos* (brother). Paul uses this word in Romans 12:10: "Be devoted to one another in brotherly love; give preference to one another in honor." And again in 1 Thessalonians 4:9, 10: "Now as to the love of the brethren, you have no need for anyone to write to you, for you yourselves are taught by God to love one another; . . ." What a tremendous compliment Paul pays these brethren. They were still babes in Christ and Paul had been with them such a short time, but they had caught on so quickly to the need to love one another.

Other writers also emphasize the need to love each other using the Greek word *philadelphia:*[2]

---

[2]Emphasis mine.

Let *love of the brethren* continue (Hebrews 13:1).

To sum up, let all be harmonious, sympathetic, *brotherly*, kindhearted, and humble in spirit (1 Peter 3:8).

And in your godliness, *brotherly kindness*, and in your brotherly kindness, love (2 Peter 1:7).

Then there are the many references that tell us to *agapao* our brethren. These find their climax in 1 John. This book alone has over fifty references to love. Let us note a few selected verses from chapter 4 that say to love our brethren:

> Beloved, let us love one another, for love is from God; and everyone who loves is born of God and knows God. The one who does not love does not know God, for God is love. . . . Beloved, if God so loved us, we also ought to love one another. No one has beheld God at any time; if we love one another, God abides in us, and His love is perfected in us. . . . If someone says, "I love God," and hates his brother, he is a liar; for the one who does not love his brother whom he has seen, cannot love God whom he has not seen. And this commandment we have from Him, that the one who loves God should love his brother also (vv. 7, 8, 11, 12, 20, 21).

However, it should not be necessary for Jesus to command us to love others in the church if we appreciate our relationship in Christ.

The church is referred to by many terms in the New Testament—"the body," "the church," "the kingdom"— but my favorite is the term "family." Paul stated he was writing to Timothy so he would know "how one ought to conduct himself in the *household of God*, which is the church of the living God" (1 Timothy 3:15). "Household" is just another way of saying "family." The church is God's family! God is our Father (1 John 3:1). Christ is our elder brother (Romans 8:29). And *we* are brothers and sisters (James 5:12).

This fact receives great emphasis in the New Testament. Those who have been scripturally baptized are called many things: "Christians" three times (Acts 11:26; 26:28; 1 Peter 4:16), "saints" several times (1 Corinthians 1:2; etc.), "members" of the body a few times (1 Corinthians 12:12, 27). But the descriptive phrase that is used more than any other is "brother" (or "brethren"). Paul himself uses the term over twenty-five times.

This should have a great effect upon our feelings toward each other. There is something special about being in the same family. Occasionally members of a family do not love each other. Cain killed Abel. There was conflict between Jacob and Esau. Absalom rebelled against his father. But as a rule, members of a family have a special attachment for each other. I have one brother, Coy, a few years younger than I. I can say uncomplimentary things about Coy, but you had better not because he is my brother! Chances are you have that kind of family, too, and understand that being members of the same family is a special thing. It is even exciting to find relatives far removed that you did not know you had.

Again I say that it should not be necessary for Christ to command us to love each other since we are brothers and sisters in Him. But the fact remains that it *is* a command.

Perhaps you respond, "I would *like* to love others in the church, but I don't know how." A number of suggestions could be given on how we can learn to love each other more. As already suggested, we need to realize the relationship we have in Christ. Again, in his first letter, John stresses that if we really appreciate what God and Christ have done for us, this *should* make us love each other.

One of the most practical lists was compiled by Bonardo Overstreet.[3] This author notes that if we would learn to love each other, we need to (1) eat together, (2) talk and listen together, (3) give and receive help, (4) work and play together, (5) learn together, (6) affirm together. Notice that these are the simplest relationships of life. The usual assumption is that we do these things when we love others. Actually we come to love others when we do these things.

This list can apply to dating, marriage, a family, or friendships. It can also apply to the church. Several of the items have special application to our relationship in Christ. We need to eat together; the early church celebrated the love feast. We need to talk together; Jesus and His disciples talked with one another as they walked along. Use every opportunity to get to know your brothers and sisters in Christ, including before and after the worship services. Do not rush in and rush out. We need to help and encourage each other; after all we are members of the same body (1 Corinthians 12). We need to learn together; as the disciples followed Jesus and learned from Him, they not only developed a relationship with the Master, they also developed a relationship with each other. Let us learn

---

[3]Prentice A. Meador, Jr., "The Gospel According to Love," in *Voices in Action*, ed. James L. Lovell (Austin, Tex.: R. B. Sweet Co., 1968), 153.

together in classes, in worship services, in other situations.

Lawns and flowerbeds do not tend themselves. Shrubs and trees do not trim themselves. And love does not just happen. Loving our brethren takes effort—but we must do it, for it is a commandment.

A NEW COMMANDMENT

But it is not just a commandment; it is a *new* commandment.

It is not new from the viewpoint of the command to love others. The Old Testament taught men to love their neighbors (Leviticus 19:18). Teachers throughout history have taught on the subject. Socrates spoke of the need for love. Buddha taught that his followers should be friends of all. But the commandment was new in that it was to be "as" Christ loved us! This love was new in *scope*, for it included all men. It was new in *self-denial*, for it was concerned about helping the other person. It was new in *service*, for it was dedicated to helping others. It was new in *sacrifice*, willing even to die for others!

So much could be said about how Christ loved us, but at this time let us note three aspects of Christ's love that would enhance our relationships in the church: Jesus' love was *ready, willing,* and *able.*

(1) Jesus' love was *ready* to believe the best.

We have seen in this study that readiness to put the best interpretation on the actions of others is one of love's great qualities. Love "believes all things" or, as the Amplified Bible puts it, love "is ever ready to believe the best of every person" (1 Corinthians 13:7).

Jesus' love has this beautiful quality. When He looked at the wavering personality of Simon, He saw the potential of a solid, unshifting commitment—and He called him Peter, the rock (Matthew 16:18). When Jesus first met John, the young man was not an apostle of love. John was ready to napalm bomb those that were not part of their company. But Jesus saw potential here, the potential of a caring heart, and He committed His mother to John's care (John 19:26, 27).

How we need this quality in the church! One lady, a member of the church, had been very outgoing. Then she stopped attending as much as she once did. She began to stay to herself. Then a handsome man started visiting her house every few days and the tongues flew—until the full story came out. She had incurable cancer, and a specialist, who was a friend, stopped by frequently to see how she was.

I think this sister made a mistake. I believe she should have shared her problem. That is what a family is for. But the point I want to make is this: How it would have helped if each one in the family had put the best possible interpretation on the situation. How simple it would have been to ask what was going on or to show concern.

After I had written and preached the sermon "The Day Christ Came (Again)" in Muskogee, Oklahoma, one of our members sent a copy to her son, who taught and preached in Arkansas. He apparently liked the lesson and used it extensively in that part of the country. After the sermon was published in tract form, I was written up as "stealing" that brother's sermon. No one ever checked with me to see what the facts were before going into print.

When we were getting ready to go to Australia, it

was mentioned that we had raised money from churches for the "Australia Bible College." This was a preacher training school, but in Australia training schools are called colleges. What we generally call "colleges" in the U.S. are called "universities" in Australia. This time I was castigated in print for "putting [secular] colleges in church budgets." Need I say it? No one checked the facts before printing the story.

I could continue with personal illustrations, but let me give one more instance, something that happened to others. Years ago, it was rumored that a large congregation in Lubbock, Texas, was getting folks to come to services by offering green stamps. What actually happened was a prankster attached an S&H Green Stamp sign to their services' sign. As soon as those in the congregation discovered it, the sign was removed. But not before several saw it. And the gossip started.

Surely it is not necessary to say that those who engage in such slander have violated many biblical principles. They have violated the principle to go to a brother if you have anything against him (Matthew 18:15). But above all, they have violated the law of love. Love is ready to believe the best of a brother.

When the accusations, the insinuations, the innuendoes begin to fly, let us pray to have the love Jesus had!

(2) Jesus' love was *willing* to overlook many faults.

Do not get ahead of me on this one. I did not say "all faults," and I did not use the word "condone." I will have more to say about such distinctions, but right now I want to stress that unless we develop the quality of being able to overlook many faults, there is no way we can get along with *anybody*.

Think of Jesus' relationship with His disciples. Call

175

to mind their weaknesses and how frequently they disappointed the Master. If Jesus had desired to do so, He could have spent every waking moment telling the disciples what was wrong with them. He would never have had time to teach the multitudes. But Jesus was patient with His special followers.

Ephesians 4:4-6 is one of the great passages on unity. It stresses that if we are to be unified, we must agree on certain great truths: one body, one Spirit, one hope, one Lord, one faith, one baptism, and one God. But notice that the passage begins in verse 1 with an emphasis on the kind of *spirit* that is necessary for unity:

> I, therefore, the prisoner of the Lord, entreat you to walk in a manner worthy of the calling with which you have been called, with all humility and gentleness, with patience, *showing forbearance to one another in love*, being diligent to preserve the unity of the Spirit in the bond of peace (Ephesians 4:1-3; emphasis mine).

Another important passage on this subject is 1 Peter 4:8: "Above all, keep fervent in your love for one another, because love covers a multitude of sins." Peter may be quoting from Proverbs 10:12: "Hatred stirs up strife, but love covers all transgressions." Many things are to be noted in the text. Peter emphasizes the importance of love when he says, *"Above all, keep fervent in your love."* He underlines the intensity of love we should have when he says, *"Keep fervent in your love for one another."* But the words I want to stress are *"Love covers a multitude of sins."*

It is a general truth that love will cause us to overlook many flaws. In almost any home there is an old toy, an outdated picture, a piece of furniture that does not quite match. Why do we keep these around? Because memories are attached to them—and love covers the defects.

Once an artist painted a picture of a friend. The man who was painted protested, "You have painted it far too fine for it to be true." "No," replied the artist, "I have simply painted it with love."

I have mentioned that I have a grandson named Seth David (notice how subtly I introduce him again). As far as I have been able to discover, he has no flaws. Even if he did, love would cover them, and he would still be the most beautiful of boys.

Now let us apply this general principle to the matter of sin. In what way does "love cover a multitude of sins"? When someone sins, if I do not love him, I will find it easy to readily condemn him. But if I do love him, among other things, I will try to understand him and try to find a reason for what he has done.

Through the years, I have done many things that have upset people. Generally, these things are more thoughtless than malicious. Often I am deep in thought and fail to notice people. Sometimes I forget to do what I said I would do. Occasionally, I hurt feelings by what I say. As a result some individuals do not care for me, and a few will have little to do with me. But there is one person to whom I have done every one of these things and more, done them over and over again, and she still sticks with me. Of course, I am talking about my wife, Jo. Why would she do this? Because "love covers a multitude of sins."

We need this attitude in the church. Most of us go through a series of stages after we become members of the church. Stage one: We think everyone in the church is perfect. Stage two: We realize that all in the church are weak and have faults. Stage three: We learn to love them anyway. Let me tell you this: If you do not make it to stage three, you will leave the church.

Is this matter of love "covering a multitude of sins" a startling new concept? No, it is just a practical application of the Golden Rule. I want others to love *me* in spite of my shortcomings. So I need to love others in spite of their shortcomings.

One peculiarity of the KJV is that occasionally it translates the word *agape* as "charity" instead of "love." One writer, however, says that when it comes to our relationships with each other, maybe "charity" is not a bad translation. We need to be charitable to one another. Like it or not, we are all charity cases.

(3) Jesus' love was *able* to forgive.

This third point ties in closely with the other two.

Jesus said to the woman taken in adultery, "Go your way. From now on sin no more" (John 8:11). On the cross He prayed, "Father, forgive them; for they do not know what they are doing" (Luke 23:34). Jesus held no grudges; no animosity was in His heart. That is the kind of love He had.

Someone objects, "But you don't know what that person has done to me! I'll never forgive, never!" I would hate to be standing near someone with an attitude like that on the day of judgment! Jesus said, "If you do not forgive men, then your Father will not forgive your transgressions" (Matthew 6:15).

It would be unrealistic to think that there would never be problems between children of God. Acts 15:39 says that "a sharp disagreement" arose between Paul and Barnabas. But even when problems arise, we

178

should not hold grudges. We should be ready to forgive. We need to love as Jesus did!

Another responds, "That's great! I guess you just want us to forget about sin, just overlook everything!" No, no. Remember that this is *agape* love. Remember that this is the love that seeks the best for the one loved. Remember that this is *tough* love. Did Jesus totally overlook sin? No. He rebuked His disciples on occasion. He called the Pharisees "serpents, . . . [a] brood of vipers" (Matthew 23:33), in other words, "snakes in the grass." He drove out the money-changers in the temple.

No passage of Scripture should ever be used in such a way to contradict another passage of Scripture. So many passages tell us to be concerned about sin. First Samuel 15 comes to mind. When Saul sinned, Samuel grieved. He cried all night. Again, 1 Peter 2:17 says that we are to "love the brotherhood," but if we are not concerned about the sins of our brothers, we do not love them.

Many passages tell us corrective discipline is sometimes necessary (1 Corinthians 5; etc.) and, in fact, that if we fail to discipline sin as we should, we do not love as we should. Note again Hebrews 12:6: "Those whom the Lord loves He disciplines, and He scourges every son whom He receives." We cannot ignore any sin that has not been repented of, for that can send a soul to hell. We do not love a person if we do not try to help him overcome sin in his life.

So I am not saying that we should ignore sin; I am saying that we can work on *how* we deal with sin. We should learn to help people in a loving way. I am especially stressing that we should work on our motivation, on our hearts. It has been said that many of us are better at the stern virtues than we are the gentle graces. We must learn to love as Jesus loved.

A DISTINGUISHING COMMANDMENT

Finally, let us notice that this is a *distinguishing* commandment. Jesus said, "By *this* all men will know that you are My disciples."

If we are proud to be members of an organization, we like to let people know. Some people display a symbol of the organization for which they work or perhaps an organization of which they are a member. On occasion I have worn the insignia of a civic organization or the badge of a society of magicians.

But Jesus said that men would not know that we are His disciples by some badge that we wear, some special uniform, or the style of our clothing or hair, but by the way we love each other.

Jesus might have specified a great many things. He could have said that men will know we are His disciples because we have been immersed in water for the remission of our sins. That is important (Acts 2:38), but it is possible to be baptized for the wrong motives. Or He might have said that men could know we are His disciples if we are able to quote many Scriptures— or any number of other things, most or all of which might be very important, even essential. Instead He said that men will know we are His followers if we have learned to love each other.

Apparently, the early church took this challenge seriously. The ancient historian Tertullian said that the world had this to say about early Christians: "Behold how they love one another; they are ready to die for one another."[4]

A word of warning: This passage is not to be taken by itself. It does not say this is how God will know we are Jesus' disciples, but rather this is how men will know. This is what *man* can see; this is what ultimately attracts or repels men. We cannot be the Lord's church unless we are right in doctrine. But the fact is that no one will be impressed about how *right* we are if we do not *love* each other. Someone made this cynical comment about members of the church: "They are a bunch of 'don't' people. They *don't* drink, they *don't* cuss, they *don't* commit adultery—and they *don't* like each other."

More than once I have gone to encourage people to return to the church and have heard stories like this: "My dad was an elder (or a preacher, a deacon, or whatever), but he abused my mom and me." Or I have gone to encourage people to obey the gospel and become members of the church to have words like these hurled at me: "Do you know 'so-and-so'? He's supposed to be a big member down there where you preach, but I've seen how he treats other people." Until we learn to love one another, our efforts at evangelism will have limited success!

May God help us to love our brethren—and to let the world see.

CONCLUSION

In this chapter, I have stressed the importance of loving others in the body of Christ. We have high-

---

[4]Quoted in *Fort Worth Christian College Lectures 1966*, 111.

lighted being ready to put the best interpretation on what our brethren do, being willing to overlook many faults, and being able to forgive. As I close, I want to ask, "What is your reaction to these teachings?" How would you complete this phrase, "Concerning the matter of brotherly love, I wish. . . ."?

Once there was a preacher who was given a new car by a member of the congregation. One day he went visiting in his new automobile. When he returned to his vehicle, a little boy in ragged clothing was admiring it. "What a great car!" the boy exclaimed. The preacher explained that he really could not afford such a car, but a brother had given it to him to use in the service of God. The youngster thought about that awhile and then said, "I wish . . . I could be a brother like that."

As we have talked about what is involved in loving our brethren, it is possible that some of us have thought, "I wish my brethren would treat *me* like that." But the response Jesus wants is, "I want to treat *my brothers and sisters* like that!"

Class Discussion and Activity

1. What effect does it have on the church when we do not love each other as we should? What effect does it have on those we are trying to influence to become Christians?
2. Are we commanded both to *agapao* (seek the best for) and *phileo* (have warm feelings toward) our brethren?
3. Discuss the passages that use a form of *philadelphia* (brotherly love). If possible, use word study books to find as many of these passages as

possible.
4. On a piece of paper, list Overstreet's six suggestions for learning to love each other. Apply these to dating, marriage, a family, and friendship. Then apply these to learning to love each other in the church. (You may want to make this a class project, putting the list on the chalkboard.)
5. Since the command to love had been given before, in what way was Jesus' command to love one another in John 13:33-35 a *new* command?
6. When we hear a story about a brother that sounds bad, do we always try to find out the facts? Then do we always put the best construction on his actions? Have you ever misjudged anyone?
7. To illustrate the fact that love overlooks many flaws, bring some memento to class that may not look attractive to others, but has special meaning to you.
8. The author gives three stages we go through when we become members of the church. Discuss these in class. Do you agree with his statement that if one does not reach stage three, he will probably quit the church? (Let each ask, "Which stage have I reached?")
9. Sometimes when people get unhappy when we try to correct them, it is because they do not like the truth. But sometimes, is it not so much *what* we say as *how* we say it? What can we do to help those we try to correct see that we are acting from the motive of love?
10. For personal examination: When we hear a discussion of how Christians ought to treat each other, what is our reaction? Is our first thought,

"I wish my brothers and sisters would treat *me* that way"? Or is it, "God, help me to treat my brothers and sisters like that"?

12
Dimensions of Love

We have talked about what love is, with an emphasis on *agape* love: Unselfish in nature, it is an act of the will, a decision, a commitment to seek the best for the one loved. We have talked about the need of loving God, our neighbors, and ourselves. We have made application to marriage preparation, our Christian homes, and our relationships with our brothers and sisters in Christ.

As we near the end of our study, we want to go to the *source* of all this, that which will really enable us to love God and others as we should. John spoke beautifully of this source in 1 John 4:19-21:

> We love, because He first loved us. If someone says, "I love God," and hates his brother, he is a liar; for the one who does not love his brother whom he has seen, cannot love God whom he has not seen. And this commandment we have from Him, that the one who loves God should love his brother also.

"We love, because He first loved us." We can preach on *agape* love until Christ comes, but we will never understand it until we see God's love for us. "We know love by this, that He laid down His life for us" (1 John 3:16). But this puts us in a quandary; there is no way we can fully know and understand what God and Jesus have done for us. Certainly there is no way I can express it as I would like. Which brings us to our text, Ephesians 3:14-21, and the paradox it presents.

In Ephesians 2, Paul speaks of salvation by grace and the fact that God's grace has been extended to all men—not just the Jews, but Gentiles also. All can be united by the cross in the one body, which is the church (Ephesians 2:16; 1:22, 23). As chapter 3 opens, Paul starts to pray for the brethren at Ephesus, most of whom were Gentile Christians. The chapter begins, "For this reason...." Then Paul pauses for a few verses to tell about his work with the Gentiles. Finally, in verse 14, he is ready for this great prayer, which climaxes the first half of the book:

> For this reason, I bow my knees before the Father, from whom every family in heaven and on earth derives its name, that He would grant you, according to the riches of His glory, to be strengthened with power through His Spirit in the inner man; so that Christ may dwell in your hearts through faith; and that you, being rooted and grounded in love, may be able to comprehend with all the saints what is the breadth and length and height and depth, and to know the love of Christ which surpasses knowledge, that you may be filled up to all the fulness of God.
> Now to Him who is able to do exceeding abundantly beyond all that we ask or think, according to the power that works within us, to

Him be the glory in the church and in Christ
Jesus to all generations forever and ever. Amen
(Ephesians 3:14-21).

There are four requests in this prayer, which tie
together:
(1) He prays that they will be strengthened in the
inner man, the soul, by the indwelling Spirit they
received when they became Christians (Acts 2:38).
(2) He prays that they will be strengthened in the
inner man, so that Christ will dwell in their hearts by
faith: as their faith increases, Christ will take up permanent residence within them.
(3) He prays that Christ will dwell in their hearts,
so that they will be rooted and grounded in love.
(4) He prays for *all* this so they will be filled with
the fullness of God. This is another way of speaking of
Christian completeness or maturity. The point of the
whole prayer is that Christians need to grow up!
The portion of the prayer that now concerns us is
the third request. In the heart of the prayer is this
request that the Ephesians will grow in love as they
come to appreciate God and Christ's love: "That you,
being rooted and grounded in love, may be able to
comprehend with all the saints what is the breadth
and length and height and depth, and to know the love
of Christ which surpasses knowledge."
Two figures of speech are blended in this request.
Roy C. Deaver, preacher trainer, calls these the agricultural and architectural figures. "Rooted ... in love"
is the agricultural figure; we need to be rooted in love
as a growing plant is rooted in the soil. "Grounded in
love" is the architectural figure; it refers to having a
firm foundation. If we *are* "rooted and grounded in

love," we will be able to do something. We will be able to comprehend the incomprehensible. We will be able to know the unknowable. "To know the love of Christ which surpasses knowledge."

Although there are depths to the subject we shall never grasp in this life, we can know some things or the words "to know" would have no meaning. Among the things we can know to some extent are the dimensions of love: "May be able to comprehend with all the saints what is the breadth and length and height and depth."

Frankly, I do not know all that is intended by the terms "breadth and length and height and depth." It may be that Paul pictures himself standing at the center of love and looking up . . . and down . . . and to one side . . . and to the other . . . and seeing no end. This would be a reference to the comprehensiveness of love, the same point he made in Romans 8:35, 37-39:

> Who shall separate us from the love of Christ? Shall tribulation, or distress, or persecution, or famine, or nakedness, or peril, or sword? . . . But in all these things we overwhelmingly conquer through Him who loved us. For I am convinced that neither death, nor life, nor angels, nor principalities, nor things present, nor things to come, nor powers, nor height, nor depth, nor any other created thing, shall be able to separate us from the love of God, which is in Christ Jesus our Lord.

When my family and I first went to Australia, we went by ship. Once I climbed to the highest point on the ship and looked out across the vast expanse of the Pacific Ocean. I looked this way and that. As far as I could see, there was only water. The illustration is not perfect, for my vision was limited. I knew that somewhere out there, there was land. But there are some similarities with Paul's statement. Paul says, in effect, "I'm in the heart of God's love. As far as I can see, there is only love. God loves me and that love knows no bounds."

That may be all Paul is saying when he uses these terms, but the dimensional terminology has fascinated scholars from the early days of the church (in the writings of Jerome) down to the present (in the writings of so many that I have studied in recent days). I would like, therefore, to use these terms to focus our thinking on how great God's love really is.

THE BREADTH OF GOD'S LOVE

We begin, as our text does, with the breadth of God's love. *How broad* is God's love? Is it so narrow that it takes in only a few, a select few, a special few? No, God's love is so broad that it takes in *all men*. We see this in the temporal world.

> . . . He Himself gives to *all* life and breath and all things (Acts 17:25; emphasis mine).

> . . . He causes His sun to rise on the evil and the good, and sends rain on the righteous and the unrighteous (Matthew 5:45).

This is just as true in the spiritual realm.

> The Lord . . . is patient toward you, not wishing for *any* to perish but for *all* to come to repentance (2 Peter 3:9; emphasis mine).

> [God] desires *all* men to be saved and to come to the knowledge of the truth (1 Timothy 2:4;

emphasis mine).

Why this is true is one of those mysteries we will never totally solve. Isaiah 44 may give some insight as God tells His people in the Old Testament why He will help them although they were not what they should be:

> But now listen, O Jacob, My servant;
> And Israel, whom I have chosen:
> Thus says the Lord who made you
> And formed you from the womb, who will help
>   you.
> "Do not fear, . . .
> For I will pour out water on the thirsty land
> And streams on the dry ground;
> I will pour out My Spirit on your offspring,
> And My blessing on your descendants; . . ."
> This one will say, "I am the Lord's"; . . .
> And another will write on his hand, "Belonging
>   to the Lord," . . .
>
> (vv. 1-3, 5)

Even though they had sinned, God was going to bless them (1) because He had made them, (2) because He had chosen them, (3) and because they were called by His name. They were His sons. Even so God has made all men, He has called all to be His people, He extends to all the possibility of being called by His name—to be His sons and daughters.

Whatever the reasons, it is emphasized again and again in the Scriptures that God's love extends to all people. Jesus "gave Himself as a ransom for all" (1 Timothy 2:6). He "taste[d] death for everyone" (Hebrews 2:9).

THE LENGTH OF GOD'S LOVE

This brings us to the length of God's love. *How far would God's love go for all men?*

My love and your love for others has limits. Jesus spoke of those limitations in John 15:13: "Greater love has no one than this, that one lay down his life for *his friends.*" (Emphasis mine.) Jesus says that a man can express no greater love than to die for a friend. But Jesus died not just for His friends, but also for His enemies. Therefore, Jesus' love is greater than the greatest. Paul picked up that thought in Romans 5 and spoke of our limitations as contrasted with God's unlimited love:

> For while we were still helpless, at the right time Christ died for the ungodly. For one will hardly die for a righteous man; though perhaps for the good man someone would dare even to die. But God demonstrates His own love toward us, in that while we were yet sinners, Christ died for us (vv. 6-8).

How far would God's love go? All the way to *the cross.* "For God *so* loved the world, that He gave His only begotten Son" (John 3:16; emphasis mine).

Here again we come to the incomprehensible and the unknowable. I can faintly comprehend the physical suffering: the hurt of the crown of thorns upon His brow, the tearing of His back with the whip, the exhaustion of His body, the overwhelming pain of the nails driven through His hands and feet, the searing agony of His lungs crying out for oxygen. But His spiritual agony as He took upon Himself the sins of each one of us (2 Corinthians 5:21), the spiritual agony reflected in the words, "My God, My God, why hast Thou forsaken Me?" (Matthew 27:46), that I cannot comprehend at all. By faith I accept it. He died for *our* sins.

> Now I make known to you, brethren, the gospel which I preached to you, which also you received, in which also you stand, . . . For I delivered to you as of first importance what I also received, that *Christ died for our sins* according to the Scriptures, and that He was buried, and that He was raised on the third day according to the Scriptures (1 Corinthians 15:1, 3, 4; emphasis mine).

Not long ago, I read a true story that touched my heart. A little boy and his dog were running and playing in the front yard when suddenly the puppy darted into the street in front of an oncoming vehicle. The little boy, seeing the danger, rushed into the street to save his pet. There was a terrible screech as the car swerved to miss them, but it was too late. Both boy and dog were killed instantly.

It was the most unusual funeral in the small town's history. Beside the beautiful casket for the child was a small wooden box and, in it, the remains of a little dog. At the cemetery, both were lowered into the grave. A tombstone was erected with the following words inscribed on it:

> He found an orphan pup one night;
> Though none could see its worth,
> He nourished it and cherished it
> As if of noble birth.
>
> He took it in and dried it off
> From cold, damp winter's rain;

And nursed it 'til its mangy coat
Was bright and thick again.

He watched that sickly dog get well;
It filled his heart with joy;
God help us all to understand
The love of a little boy.

The unique service closed with these words: "*Jesus loves us like this boy loved his dog.*"
That is the length of God's love.

THE DEPTH OF GOD'S LOVE

Next there is the depth of God's love. *How deep* could God's love go? We have suggested that His love is broad enough to include all men, but it is hard not to think that surely some get so mired in sin, get so deep in guilt, that not even God's love can reach them. The beautiful truth is that God's love can reach to the depths and rescue the most hardened of sinners.

Paul considered himself the prime object lesson of this truth. In 1 Timothy 1:15, he refers to himself as the "foremost" of sinners, but Jesus still saved him! Another illustration of this truth would be the woman Jesus talked to at the well of Samaria in John 4. Few of us would consider her a "prime prospect" for conversion. Her life was totally messed up; we would probably have thought she could not be reached. But Jesus' love and concern awakened something within her. Let us call it hope. God's love reaches down into Texas, Oklahoma, Australia, India—into the wealthiest and the poorest parts of each town, into the jails, into the houses of prostitution—and says, "There is hope."

The fact that God's love could reach anyone, no matter how deep in sin, amazed early Christians. It amazed Paul. He said, ". . . I live by faith in the Son of God, who loved *me*, and delivered Himself up for *me*" (Galatians 2:20; emphasis mine). It amazed the apostle John. Four times he referred to himself as the disciple Jesus loved.

An old Indian chief constantly spoke of Jesus and what He meant to him. A friend asked, "Why do you talk so much about this Jesus?" The chief did not reply, but rather gathered some sticks and bits of grass and made a circle of them. In the circle he placed a caterpillar. Without a word he set the sticks and grass on fire. They watched the caterpillar. As the fire spread around the circle, the caterpillar began to crawl rapidly, seeking a way of escape. As the fire advanced, the little creature raised its head as high as it could. Then the old Indian stooped down and extended his finger to the caterpillar. It crawled up his finger. The chief gently put it in a safe place and spoke for the first time: "That is what Jesus did for me. I was lost in sin. I was trapped. My condition was hopeless. Then the Lord stooped down and lifted me out of my pit of sin and shame. How can I help but love Him and speak of His wondrous love and care?"

The chief's illustration was not accidental as he compared himself to a caterpillar, a worm-like creature. Each of us can say, "I was *nothing*—but Jesus loved me and Jesus rescued me."

THE HEIGHT OF GOD'S LOVE

Finally there is the height of God's love. We can

know the height of a thing by looking up. I can still remember my first trip to Oklahoma City from a tiny Oklahoma town and looking up at the tall buildings (some were fifteen to twenty stories high!). I came home with sun-burned tonsils. Since then I have looked up at much taller buildings, such as the Empire State Building in New York City, the Sears Tower in Chicago, and the Center Point Tower in Sydney, Australia. But none of them compares to the height of God's love.

Many suggestions have been given as to what exactly is meant by the "height" of God's love. Love is so high, we "can't get over it" (Romans 8:39). Love is so high, it reaches into heaven. God is there, and "God is love" (1 John 4:8, 16). And each member of the Godhead loves the other members of the Godhead (John 17:24).

My personal favorite, however, is the idea that love *lifts us up*. Jesus said, "And I, if I be lifted up from the earth, will draw all men to Myself" (John 12:32). We sing, "Love lifted me! When nothing else could help, love lifted me." In this life, God's love lifts me from the guilt of my sin as I respond to Him in loving obedience, and someday that love will lift me into *heaven*, into His presence!

CONCLUSION

But after we have explored these fascinating words, "breadth," "length," "depth," and "height," we must admit there is much we cannot know about them. But this much we can know: Whatever the significance of the words, they find their significance in *the cross*. The

Latin word for "cross" is *crux*. We speak of "the crux of the matter," meaning the center or heart of the matter. The cross is the center of God's love.

Even if mysteries are here we cannot fathom, there are still lessons for us to learn:

(1) Let us appreciate how much God loves us personally. Karl Barth, the renowned theologian, was once asked the greatest thought he ever had. He replied, "Jesus loves me, this I know, for the Bible tells me so." There is no grander thought than this: "Jesus loves *me*." Some people today say, "No one loves me." Jesus loves you; God loves you. They are on your side, and they will help you.

(2) We need to imitate God's love. We need to learn what love really is—and then practice it. Let us put some *breadth* into our love and love all men. Let us put some *length* into our love and really sacrifice and be unselfish. Let us put some *depth* into our love and love people because they need it, whether they deserve it or not. Let us put some *height* into our love and strive to lift people up by our love, not drag them down.

(3) Although we can never fully apprehend and comprehend all the aspects of God's love, let us still take full advantage of it by our response of loving obedience. I do not comprehend electricity, but I do know how to turn on a light switch. I will never fully understand God's love, but I can still benefit from it by loving obedience (John 14:15; 1 John 5:3).

Class Discussion and Activity

1. Study the prayer in Ephesians 3:14-21 in depth. Note how the four requests tie together and

how each leads to the next.

2. What do you think is meant by "the breadth" of love?
3. Study Isaiah 44:1-3, 5. Especially note the three reasons God was going to bless them. Apply these to the Israelites, and then apply these reasons to us.
4. What do you think is meant by "the length" of love?
5. Discuss the physical suffering of Jesus on the cross.
6. Discuss the spiritual suffering of Jesus on the cross.
7. What do you think is meant by "the depth" of love?
8. Most of us have John 3:16 memorized. How about memorizing Galatians 2:20? It is even more personal: Jesus "loved *me*."
9. What do you think is meant by "the height" of love?
10. Discuss how *we* can add "breadth," "length," "depth," and "height" to *our* love.

13
Let's Get Serious

Jacob was returning home. He was full of apprehension, for he would soon be face to face with Esau, the one whom he had cheated out of the birthright. The night before he met Esau was a terrifying night for Jacob. The Bible says he wrestled all night with an angel (Genesis 32:24; see also Hosea 12:3, 4). He did not win the match, but neither did he lose.[1] In fact he received a blessing because of it. When day was approaching, the angel said, "Let me go, for the dawn is breaking," and Jacob replied, "I will not let you go unless you bless me" (Genesis 32:26). Then the angel changed his name to "Israel," which means "prince of

---

[1]The reference in Hosea says Jacob had power over the angel and "prevailed," but the point seems to be that, considering his opponent, fighting to a draw was quite an accomplishment. Since we are talking about an opponent with unlimited resources, we assume that all of the angel's strength was not used, that Jacob was *allowed* to continue the struggle all night. All of this was obviously an object lesson for Jacob's benefit. What that object lesson might have been does not concern us at this time.

God"[2] (Genesis 32:27, 28).

For twelve chapters, we have been wrestling with the biblical concept of love. It has been a humbling experience; the subject is overwhelming. But we have tried to hang on, not to turn loose. I will not be so bold as to say we have won; we have not begun to exhaust the subject. But, on the other hand, I do not believe we have lost. My life has been blessed as a result of the effort; I hope yours has too.

Now that we have come to the last chapter, let me share with you why I call this series "Getting Serious About Love." That phrase has a double significance. First, I want to emphasize that this is a *serious* attempt to grasp the biblical concept of love. There is a need for teaching on love that primarily aims for the *heart*. It would be foolish to deny this when in recent years so many "feel good" books on love have been best sellers. Hopefully, however, there is also the need for teaching on love that starts with the *head* and progresses to the heart. From time to time it is good to get back to basics on the subject, to re-emphasize the biblical basis for our teaching on the topic.

The phrase is also a play on words. Regarding the subject of love, the word "serious" can be used not only to refer to an in-depth *approach*, but also to an in-depth *relationship*. The young girl confides, "I think I'm getting serious about him." When we see a couple of marriageable age dating with regularity, we ask, "Are they getting serious?" I hope that, as a result of this book, we will all "get serious" about God and each other.

---

[2]There are also other possibilities, such as "one who strives with God."

That is the emphasis of this final chapter: Let us get serious!

WE HAVE BEEN SERIOUS
IN LEARNING ABOUT LOVE

We have been very serious in our study of love.

We started by stressing the importance of our subject with a study called "Still Number One!" At the end of the great love chapter of the Bible, Paul said, "But now abide faith, hope, love, these three; but the greatest of these is love" (1 Corinthians 13:13).

Faith, hope, and love might be thought of as "the big three" of our Christian lives. Paul said,

> We give thanks to God always for all of you, making mention of you in our prayers; constantly bearing in mind your work of *faith* and labor of *love* and steadfastness of *hope* in our Lord Jesus Christ in the presence of our God and Father (1 Thessalonians 1:2, 3; emphasis mine).

Each of these qualities is so important. Without faith we cannot please God (Hebrews 11:6). Hope is the anchor of the soul (Hebrews 6:19); hope keeps us going. How significant then is the statement that "the *greatest* of these is love."

Most people have some understanding of how important love is. One person said, "Love may or may not make the world go around, but one thing is sure: It makes the trip worthwhile."

Next, to lay a background for our series, we focused on a study of the Greek words translated "love" in a chapter on "The Greeks Have a Word for It." We use the word "love" in a superficial way today. We speak of loving everything from soup to nuts, from people to petunias. We talk about falling in love as though it were a well-heated swimming pool.

To sharpen our thinking on love, we discussed the four Greek words for love: (1) *Eros* refers to "physical attraction"; we called this "Strawberry Shortcake Love." (2) *Storge* is "family love"; we designated this "Aunt Minnie Love." (3) *Philia* is the word for "friendship love"; this is "Bowling Team Love." (4) *Agape* is an act of the will; this we named "Rain-on-the-Just-and-the-Unjust Love." We focused our attention on *philia* and *agape*. *Eros* is never used in the New Testament, and *storge* is seldom used, but *philia* or *agape* is found on almost every page.

Our great emphasis, however, was the word *agape*. It is the special word for "love" in the New Testament. It is the word John used when he said, "God is love" (1 John 4:8, 16). It is the word used in 1 Corinthians 13, the love chapter of the Bible. To stress the distinctive qualities of *agape*, we had a chapter on "Tough Love." We looked at some of the qualities of *agape*: It is unconditional love. It is active love. It is loyal love. It is love that does not quit. One of its most distinctive qualities is that it is unselfish. It is not primarily interested in getting; it *is* concerned with giving. A story by Victor Hugo illustrates this quality:

> After the revolution, a French mother was driven from her home with her three children, including an infant. She had wandered through the woods and fields for several days. She and her three children had lived on roots and leaves. On the third morning, they had hidden in some bushes on the approach of some soldiers and a sergeant. The sergeant ordered a soldier to find

out what was stirring in the bushes; he prodded the mother and her three children out. They were brought to the sergeant's side, and he saw in an instant that they were starving; he gave them a long loaf of brown French bread. The mother took it eagerly, like a famished animal, broke it into two pieces, giving one piece to one child and the other to the second child.

"She has kept none for herself," grumbled the sergeant.

"Because she is not hungry," said a soldier.

"Because she is a mother," said the sergeant.[3]

But, although one can list characteristics of *agape* love, it is hard to define. Even in the longest and most complete treatment of it in 1 Corinthians 13, Paul does not attempt to define *agape*, but rather describes it. Since that great chapter is so central to the subject, we devoted two chapters to it.

The title of the first we took from the last verse of 1 Corinthians 12: "The 'More Excellent Way.'" Paul gives three reasons love is the more excellent way: The first is its *superiority*. Paul lets us know that no matter how great a man's abilities, without love, he is "nothing."

If I had the abilities that are listed in 1 Corinthians 13:1-3, I would think I was "something." I have always admired people who had the gift of learning foreign languages. I do not have that gift; I lack the ear for it. If I could speak in a dozen languages, I would think I was something. I have a library of several thousand volumes. I have not read a fraction of what is in those volumes and have retained little of what I have read. If

---

[3]From *Ninety-Three*; quoted by Charles Allen in *Faith, Hope, and Love* (Old Tappan, N.J.: Fleming H. Revell Co., 1982), 120-21.

I knew everything in those books, I would think I was something. Life is full of mysteries. If I could solve but one of them, I would think I was something. But Paul said that no matter what my accomplishments, *without love*, I am a nothing, a naught, a zero, a zip.

The third reason love is the "more excellent way" is because of its *stability*. Other things pass away, but love lasts. "But now *abide* faith, hope, love, these three." If we were to make a list of the things that most concern us and take the most of our time, a high percentage would be things that are temporary, that relate to the here and now. The *abiding* qualities are faith, hope, and love, "and the greatest of these is love."

Going back to the second reason, love is the "more excellent way" because of its *superlatives*, its special qualities that are listed in 1 Corinthians 13:4-7. Since these are the heart of Paul's discussion of *agape* love, we took an entire chapter to discuss them, in a study on "God's Answer to Many Problems." Love is patient, kind, and not jealous. Love is humble, courteous, unselfish, and good-natured. Love believes the best. Love is concerned. How my life needs such qualities!

Having attempted to establish what *agape* love is, we then turned to "Priorities of Love." When the scribe asked Jesus what the great commandment was, He replied:

> "You shall love the Lord your God with all your heart, and with all your soul, and with all your mind." This is the great and foremost commandment. The second is like it, "You shall love your neighbor as yourself." On these two commandments depend the whole Law and the Prophets (Matthew 22:37-39).

The first priority is to *love God* with all our hearts, souls, and minds. To love God with the heart is to love God with the emotions. Our love for God should touch our hearts as the love for Jesus touched the heart of the woman who washed His feet with her tears (Luke 7:38). To love God with the soul is to love Him with our very being, to love Him with our all. To love God with the mind is to love Him with our intellect. When Muslims enter their mosques to worship Allah, they believe they should leave their shoes outside. When some of us who are Christians come to worship God, apparently we feel we should leave our minds outside. But not so; we are to love God with our minds.

At this point in our study, we wrestled with the concept of loving self as implied in the second commandment: "You shall love your neighbor *as yourself*." This chapter, which was intended to provoke thought, was titled "Self-Love Vs. Selfishness." It attempted to find a middle ground between extremes. It was noted that biblically, loving self is little concerned with having "a good self-image" or with feeling good about one's self. While we as Christians have many reasons for having a sense of self-worth, we need always to be aware of the dangers of the emphasis on self found in much modern teaching. In his book, *Learning to Love*, popular speaker Willard Tate addresses these dangers:

> The really scary thing about the self-image movement is that if you get to liking yourself and the way you are along the lines it teaches, the logical progression of thought takes you to the point of believing you don't need a Savior. *I'm Okay, You're Okay* was the title of one hugely successful book. And if we're okay, why do we

need Jesus? Well, the truth is that apart from Jesus, I'm *not* okay, and neither are you. . . .

We have a fatal disease, and it's known as sin, not lack of self-esteem. And it's only when we admit our neediness, repent, and come to the Lord on His terms for His forgiveness that we have any hope.[4]

After struggling with the phrase "as yourself," we turned to the real thrust of the second commandment: "*Love your neighbor* as yourself." For many of us this is "Love Put to the Test." In the parable of the Good Samaritan, Jesus left no doubt that the term "neighbor" includes all men (Luke 10). In fact, in the Sermon on the Mount, Christ stressed that we are even to love our enemies (Matthew 5:44ff.). This forced us to re-examine what *agape* really means: not necessarily "feeling good" about the one loved, but rather "seeking the best" for the one loved. Instead of getting back at our enemies, we should seek to help them, lift them up, and, if possible, win them by our love. The great object lesson of this kind of love is Jesus on the cross, praying, "Father, forgive them; for they do not know what they are doing" (Luke 23:34).

When he was a boy, the gifted black tenor Roland Hayes heard an old preacher expound on Jesus during His trials and death. The minister closed with the words, "No matter how mean they were, He never said a mumberlin' word, not a word." Years later Roland Hayes stood before a hostile Nazi audience in Berlin's Beethoven Hall. As the insults and hisses grew louder and louder, he became angrier and angrier. Then he remembered the sermon of long ago:

---

[4]Willard Tate, *Learning to Love* (Nashville, Tenn.: Gospel Advocate Co., 1988), 59.

"He never said a mumberlin' word, not a word." He stood there in silence, praying, until the crowd grew quiet. Then he began to sing. He won them by his singing, without "a mumberlin' word."

But we did not want to leave the matter of loving others in the area of theory. We next had three chapters of practical application. We started with the important subject of marriage in a chapter called "Two to Get Ready." We returned to the Greek words *eros*, *philia*, and *agape* and the part each should play in the preparation for and preservation of a good marriage. It was stressed that far too many marriages today are based primarily on *eros*, physical attraction.

In his book on *Happiness in the Home*, educator Harold Hazelip asserts that this is a major factor in the failure of many marriages.[5] He notes that the French writer Denis de Rougemont, in his *Love in the Western World*, observes that there is a direct correlation between the high divorce rate and the fact that we "marry for love." (By "love," we generally mean "romantic love," which, in a great many cases is a synonym for *eros*.) The noted author C. S. Lewis asserted that *eros* can unite people who are not suited for each other. A young man is likely to conclude, "Better to be miserable with her than to be happy without her."

In our chapter on marriage, we stressed that before two get married, *eros* needs to develop into *philia*, friendship; and *philia* needs to develop into *agape*, commitment. As long as a couple keeps commitment love, they can weather any storm within or without their marriage.

---

[5]Harold Hazelip, *Happiness in the Home* (Grand Rapids, Mich.: Baker Book House, 1985), 115-16.

We then turned from marriage to the family, emphasizing that love is "The Heart of the Home." Our approach was simple: everyone in the home needs to love everyone else in the home.

Our problem today seems to be "spiritual TB": we are *Too Busy*. To borrow the phrasing of 1 Kings 20:40, we are just "busy here and there." We get too busy to say, "I love you." We get too busy to be patient. We get too busy to work out differences while they are small. We get too busy to show how much we care.

Love in the home needs to start with dad and mom. "Husbands, love your wives, just as Christ also loved the church and gave Himself up for her" (Ephesians 5:25). I read recently of a man who had a peculiar habit, but we husbands could learn from him.

> For years, he had a special date with his wife every Thursday night. He would come home in the afternoon, shave and shower, put on his best suit, and go out in his car and leave. In a little while, he would come back and ring the doorbell. His wife would greet him at the door, and they would sit for a while in the living room and talk. Then they would go out to dinner and a show together. They would drive up to the front; he would escort her to the door, kiss her goodnight, and then go drive his car into the garage and come in through the back door.[6]

From the home, we went to another practical area: the need to love each other in the church. The title of our chapter, "The Badge of Discipleship," was taken from Jesus' statement in John 13:35: "By this all men will know that you are My disciples, if you have love for one another."

---

6 Allen, 157.

Unfortunately, it is *not* always possible to tell that we are Jesus' disciples by the way we get along with each other. Once it was announced at the end of a worship service that a group that was working on a project would meet at a certain sister's home. After the service, a woman who was on the same committee huffed up to the preacher and said, "I am *not* going over to her house—not after the way she treated me in the past!" The preacher looked at her for a while and then asked, "How long have you been part of this congregation?" "Twenty-seven years," she answered. The preacher then named the godly men who had filled the pulpit during those twenty-seven years. "Dear sister," he said sadly, "have you heard nothing in those twenty-seven years?"

If we are ever to learn how to get along as brethren, one of our great needs is to learn to *forgive*. Jesus taught us to pray, "Forgive us our debts, as we also have forgiven our debtors" (Matthew 6:12). For some reason we equate a forgiving spirit with weakness. We seem to feel that we are condoning wrong if we forgive. We think that in some way we have lost and the other person has won if we forgive. But when Jesus prayed on the cross, "Father, forgive them," He showed strength and not weakness. He did not condone evil. Rather He saw a great victory.

It is the cross that ultimately defines and demonstrates love. So as we neared the end of our series, we returned to the source of all love in our chapter on "Dimensions of Love." John said, "We love, because He first loved us" (1 John 4:19). The only perfect, totally unselfish example of *agape* love is God.

Several years ago John M. Templeton, an American financier-philanthropist, financed a religious Nobel prize worth $88,400 annually to be awarded to anyone who was "instrumental in widening man's knowledge of the love of God."[7] I do not know if anyone has been awarded that prize, but I doubt that anyone has ever improved on God's own expressions of His love. Every blade of grass, every rainbow, every baby's smile declares that our God loves (James 1:17). But the great demonstration of His love is the cross. "God so loved the world, that He gave His only begotten Son, . . ." (John 3:16).

The AIDS epidemic continues to spread. Millions of tax dollars are being spent in treatment and in the attempt to find a cure. Let us imagine that one day soon the cure is discovered: If a certain kind of blood can be found, it can be used to make the antidote. Then a short time later, there is a knock at your door. A worldwide search has revealed that only one person in all the world has that blood. Your baby boy, your only son. To develop the antidote will take every ounce of blood in his body. To save all those with AIDS, your son will have to give his life! Could you agree to that? Could I? I doubt it.

But we had a disease far more deadly than AIDS, brought on by our own willfulness, a disease called "sin"—and the only cure was the blood of God's only Son. How could God pay that price? I do not know; I can never understand it; but I thank Him that He did it.

The incomprehensible nature of that gesture of love was the theme as we discussed "the breadth and length and height and depth" of the sacrifice of Jesus

---

[7]Reported in *Christianity Today*; quoted in *Encyclopedia of 7,700 Illustrations* (Rockville, Md.: Assurance Publishers, 1979), 493.

on the cross (Ephesians 3:18ff.).

That brings us to this final chapter. We have been most serious in studying about love. Now let us get serious about living the love we have been studying about.

LET'S GET SERIOUS ABOUT *LIVING* LOVE

I came across a cartoon recently that showed a preacher leaning on the pulpit saying, "This is the fourth sermon on the transforming power of the gospel. Why do you look like the same old bunch?" Probably the minister was expecting too much (no doubt, he looked like the same old preacher), but his question has a certain validity. After studying the subject of love together, has it made a difference in our lives? Or do *we* still "look like the same old bunch"?

After Paul's great chapter on love, he urged his readers: "Pursue love" (1 Corinthians 14:1). "Pursue" translates a Greek word that means "to follow *eagerly*, endeavor *earnestly* to acquire; . . . to *press* forwards."[8] (Emphasis mine.) This is a strong word, an active word. It is not enough merely to learn about love; we need to *do* something.

Ever since I started this study, I have been struggling with a question: "Why is there so little genuine love in the world?" We all seem to agree that "what the world needs now is love, sweet love." Anytime anyone talks about the need for more love, we all nod our heads vigorously. But at the same time the world

_____

[8]"*Diōkō*," in *Analytical Greek Lexicon* (London: Samuel Bagster & Sons Ltd., 1971 reprint), 104.

in general seems to be getting more mean spirited. Why is that?

I have come to the conclusion that what many of us mean when we say, "The world needs love," is, "*I* need love. *I'm* lonely. *I* need someone to understand. *I* need someone to be nice to *me*." When our oldest daughter, Cindy, was just a tiny thing and learned about sharing in her Bible class, for weeks she went around saying, "Share with *me*; share with *me*." I fear that after talking about the need for love, many of us are standing around saying, "Love me; be nice to me." If that is true, it is little wonder that the world does not become more loving.

But let us get closer to home. After reading the previous twelve chapters, most of us probably have a pretty good idea concerning what it means to be a loving person. So why are you not more loving? Why am *I* not more loving? *Because to become more loving, I would have to change, and I do not like to change.*

If I were speaking to a group and asked for a show of hands of all those who would like to be better, most people would hold up their hands. But the truth of the matter is, deep inside we do not want to be better, because to become better we have to change. *And change involves pain.* To change we have to get out of our comfort zones, and very few people really like to get out of their comfort zones. If you do not believe me, try to do something as simple as getting people to sit in a part of a church auditorium other than the one they have sat in for the last ten or so years. Regardless of how much lip-service we give to change, even needed change, the fact is "we like things as they are."

The final challenge of this book, therefore, is to make some positive moves toward getting out of our spiritual comfort zones, to hurt a little if need be to become more loving people, to love God more and to love others more.

First, let us get more serious about loving God.

After Jesus had been raised from the dead, He appeared to Peter and several other disciples beside the Sea of Galilee. Standing on the seashore, Jesus looked at the man who had denied Him three times and asked him a series of questions:

> . . . Jesus said to Simon Peter, "Simon, son of John, do you love Me more than these?" He said to Him, "Yes, Lord; You know that I love You." He said to him, "Tend My lambs.' He said to him again a second time, "Simon, son of John, do you love Me?" He said to Him, "Yes, Lord; You know that I love You." He said to him, "Shepherd My sheep." He said to him the third time, "Simon, son of John, do you love Me?" Peter was grieved because He said to him the third time, "Do you love Me?" And he said to Him, "Lord, You know all things; You know that I love You." Jesus said to him, "Tend My sheep" (John 21:15-17).

For a moment imagine that you are standing where Peter stood. The Lord is looking into your eyes. Perhaps His hands are upon your shoulders. He looks deeply into your soul as He speaks your name and then asks, "Do you love Me?" Like Peter, you are keenly aware that you have let Him down time and time again. What would your answer be? What would my answer be if Jesus asked me that question?

Love for God, love for Jesus, is the beginning point of love. Do I really love God? Or do I just *say* I love God?

Several times in this book, we have discussed the

shallowness of *eros* love, love so-called that is infatuated, but not committed—a "love" that is self-centered. Our application has been to human relationships, especially to marriage. Author Charles Allen makes the point, however, that it is also possible to have this kind of "love" toward God:

> We pretend we love God, but often it is with an ulterior motive. It isn't God we want—instead we want peace of mind, or power in life, or the answer to our prayers, or we want to escape hell, or we want God's providence. And, so often, when something upsetting happens to us, we turn away from our faith in bitter resentment.[9]

Do we really love God. Are we really committed to God? Are we committed to obeying Him no matter what? Are we committed to staying with Him no matter what? Can it be *seen* in our lives that we love Him?

When Jesus first asked Peter if he loved Him, the full question was, "Do you love Me *more than these?*" "These" in Peter's case referred to nets, boats, fish, all the things that had been a vital part of Peter's life in the past. What would "these" refer to in your case? In mine? What things are so important to me, so much a part of my life, maybe so much a part of my past? Possessions? Family? Occupation? Friends? Position? You may want to examine yourself for a moment and fill in the blanks. Then again picture Jesus looking into your eyes with the searching question, "Do you love Me more than all these?" What would we say? Is God really *first* in our lives and in our affections?

Years later, the one to whom Jesus first asked this

9Allen, 148.

question wrote two letters to fellow Christians. In his first letter, he had this to say concerning his readers' relationship with God: "Though you have not seen Him, you love Him, . . ." (1 Peter 1:8). May this be true of each of us! Let us get more serious about loving God.

Let us also get more serious about loving one another.

After Peter was able to answer, in effect, "Yes, I do love You," Jesus then said, "Take care of My sheep." In fact He said it three times.

Jesus is so practical. It is easy to *say,* "Yes, I love You, Jesus." Jesus says, "Prove it by taking care of others." Remember: ". . . the one who does not love his brother whom he has seen, cannot love God whom he has not seen" (1 John 4:20).

Did Peter get the point? Let us refer to Acts 3. The events described there occur sometime after the scene on the seashore. Jesus has returned to His Father. The church has been established. Now Peter and a fellow apostle are on their way to the temple, probably to preach the good news of Jesus. When they reach the Beautiful Gate, a lame man asks for alms. Peter has to say, "I do not possess silver and gold" (v. 6). Is that not sad? He has nothing to put in the man's cup.

But there is something marvelous about love. *Love always has something to give.* It may not be what was asked for, it may not be what is expected, but love always has something to give. Peter says, "But what I do have I give to you." That is all God asks. That we give what we do have. God does not expect more than we are able to do, but He *does* expect *all* that we are able to do. We may not have a million dollars to give to people, but we do have words of love, acts of kindness, and a direct line to the ear of God on their behalf. Let us give what we have.

When Peter gave what he had, the lame man was healed and began to leap and praise God (vv. 6-8)! How many people might be healed spiritually and emotionally if we would learn to give what we have—and to give it in a loving way? "Feed My sheep," said Jesus. "Tend My [little] lambs. Shepherd My sheep."

Let us remember: Love takes care of any need. Love takes care of every need. Someone has said that love goes through the whole spiritual alphabet. Let me show you what that means. Love is:

Accepting: If I love you, I accept you as you are.

Believing: If I love you, I believe you are special.

Caring: If I love you, I care when you hurt.

Desiring: If I love you, I desire what is best for you.

Enduring: If I love you, I will not give up on you.

Forgiving: If I love you, I will forgive your sins and offenses.[10]

You can take it from there.

CONCLUSION

We come to the close of our study. I would love to hand you your BSL degree right now (that is, the Brotherhood of Serious Love). But the course is not over. We have had the instruction and the assignments have been made, but now you and I must do the homework. May God bless us as we do that.

Maybe it is because the world is changing so much. Maybe it is because I am getting older. But I have a

---

[10]Compiled and adapted from a variety of sources.

strong feeling that time is growing short—and we are still not what we should be. *I am not what I should be; I am not the loving person I should be.*

Willard Tate tells a sad story, the story of a young man.[11] He went into the Marines because his father had been in the Marines. But the young man's heart really was not in it. He turned into a discipline problem and was dishonorably discharged. The father's heart was crushed, and he disowned his son. The young man moved to another part of the country and built a new life for himself, but he was always heavy at heart because he did not have his father's love and approval. One day he learned that his father was seriously ill, and he rushed to him. But when he reached his father's bedside, the father was already unconscious, and he died without regaining consciousness. The sad story ends with the boy weeping because he knew he would never hear those words that meant all was well between him and his father.

It is a story with an ending that breaks my heart. But let me give you a more tragic ending: What if we end our days on earth without ever saying those words and doing those things that would reconcile us with our God? Without ever saying those words and doing those things that will let others know how much we love them? May God help us to get serious about love!

---

[11] Tate, 28. The story is taken from *The Blessing* by Smalley and Trent.

Class Discussion and Activity

1. Review the previous twelve chapters. Did you find any particular chapter especially helpful? Share one insight that you gained—or had reaffirmed.
2. Briefly discuss the importance of faith. Do the same for hope. Then discuss the significance of this statement: "But the *greatest* of these is *love.*"
3. Do you agree with the statement that a direct correlation exists between the divorce rate and the fact that we "marry for love"? (What, however, do most people *mean* by the word "love"?)
4. In class, first ask the men: What did you think about the way the husband mentioned in this chapter "dated" his wife? Then ask the women the same question. Discuss ideas for keeping love alive in a marriage.
5. Why do we find it hard to forgive? Is it possible that some of us equate forgiving someone with weakness . . . or the condoning of wrong . . . or letting the other person "win"?
6. Discuss what it cost God to give up His Son to die on the cross. How hard would it be to give up an only son or daughter?
7. Why is there so little love in the world? Discuss the author's suggestions. Do you have any other suggestions?
8. Is it true that most of us do not like to *change,* even when we know we should? Can you think of any examples of people resisting change?
9. For self-examination: Why do I serve God? Because of what He can give me? Or because I love Him?

10. The lesson asserts that "love always has some-thing to give." List some of the things love has to give even if it has no money.
11. Optional: Try to finish the alphabetical listing started in the chapter. Begin with "G" and start listing characteristics of love that start with each letter of the alphabet.